Date Your Spouse From Your House

52 Budget-Friendly Ways to Go Out While Staying In

Sarah Excell

Dedicated to my parents, Glen and Kim Thomas, who can still be found together every Friday night after 40 years of marriage.

A Look at the Cards

First Impressions

It was three years and one baby into our marriage when my husband and I began to notice we had unintentionally stopped paying attention to each other. It's easy to understand why. Becoming new parents is an all-consuming adjustment.

If our son was awake, we were catering to his every need. If he was asleep, we were scouring the internet for cyber advice to make sure our parental practices were as up-to-date as possible. Our life's purpose revolved around trying our hardest not to mess up as new parents, which left us with mere scraps of energy for each other by the end of each day.

As soon as our baby was in bed every night, our evening ritual was to quietly collapse in opposite corners of the house. My husband, Jeff, would sit with a crossword puzzle in the living room while I disappeared to the bedroom to indulge in the newest episode of *The Bachelor*.

We recognized, and then immediately tried to ignore, the nagging feeling that we weren't putting much effort into nourishing our marriage. Instead, we'd convince ourselves that we'd focus more on our marriage when our baby was older and we weren't so exhausted.

Over time, worrisome thoughts began to prod me during my late-night TV binging. I considered how parents to one baby often quickly become parents to two babies. I mentally walked the path my husband and I were headed down and found our dreams of one day reconnecting inevitably and repeatedly overrun by our own children. In a paranoid panic, I convinced myself that not only was I floundering through motherhood, I was potentially sabotaging my relationship with my husband along the way.

The crowning moment of my I'm-a-neglectful-spouse panic attack happened when a haunting image crept into my mind. It was the vivid memory of a cross stitch, crafted tenderly by my mother, that seemed to have no other purpose than to serve as the final dagger to my heart in this humbling moment of self-assessment. Its timeless words pierced my guilty conscience: "The most important thing a father can do for his children is to love their mother."

I crashed my head on my pillow in defeat. I reflected on how we had spent our child's entire existence trying to use the most effective disciplining tactics, the most organically processed baby food, and the most politically correct sleep training methods. We'd doted on him, giving him all the best books, toys, and gadgets to make sure he developed and excelled in the right ways.

In the meantime, one of the most important things he would need to learn—how to love, have respect for, and cherish someone—was quickly becoming overshadowed by all our other concerns for him.

I turned my attention back to *The Bachelor* in a subtle attempt to drown my thoughts out in a wave of reality TV. *KNOCK, KNOCK, KNOCK!* The front door of the mansion appeared on the screen, followed by a swarm of singles shrieking, "DATE CARD!!"

I rolled my eyes at the giddiness, the excitement, and the flirty hand-written notes. The whole scene was practically mocking me in my moment of despair. "Look at us," the contestants gloated with their date-ready hair, their optimism towards romance, and their hyperactive eyelashes. "Love is literally knocking on our front door!"

When the host of the show, Chris Harrison, appeared on the screen, he seemed to smugly speak directly to me. "Look at what you've lost, Sarah. You let it all slip away. Your life would be completely void of romance if it weren't for the times you tune into this show. I'll get out of your way now so you can continue watching what you'll never have again."

"WHAT DO YOU KNOW?!?" I screamed back at Chris, loose chocolate chips flying out of my mouth from the cookie dough I'd been mindlessly eating. In a rage, I turned off the TV and retreated into my bed.

Chris Harrison's imaginary taunts, paired with the wise words of my mother's cross stitch, swirled in my mind until they gradually aligned. In a moment of sudden clarity and with a burst of excitement I resolved, "I don't need Chris! I have me! I'm just as capable of planning a date as Chris Harrison!" As the idea solidified, I puffed up with determination, "I don't even need a babysitter. I can date my husband right from our house!"

On a secret mission, I eagerly sent my husband off to work the next day. I began to trudge through the realities of trying to imitate reality TV as I planned to date my husband without the remote paradise islands, the on-demand helicopter pilots, and the expert team of romance manufacturers. What we did have access to was a tight budget, a toddler, and luckily, a healthy dose of resourcefulness.

I figured the best place to start our at-home dating was to reenact one of our first premarital dates when we made a cherry pie together. I strategically placed a date card on the kitchen counter for Jeff to discover when he arrived home from work that evening. (See Chris Harrison? I told you I didn't need you.)

"Being with you is as easy as pie," Jeff read the date card with some confusion. "What's this?"

"It's a date card." I said.

"What's a date card?"

I glared at him for not being more familiar with the vocabulary of my favorite TV show. "It's me asking you out on a date! With a little hint about what we'll be doing on our date." With an eager smile, he disappeared to get ready for his one-on-one.

After our son was soundly asleep, I walked out of the house, positioned myself on our front porch, closed the door, and knocked in a hopeful effort to fully capture the dating experience.

Maybe that's what you'll do, too, as the spirit of dating your spouse catches hold of you. Because once you realize you can still have fun with the one you love from the confines of your own home (and budget), you might find yourself doing silly things like picking your date up from your own house.

Our first night of homebound dating turned into two, then three, then more. Rather than draining us of our energy like we feared it would, making time for each other proved to be the secret weapon to energize our week. Date night gave us something exciting to look forward to, it gave us opportunities to try new things together, and it momentarily removed us from our day-to-day cares.

The best part of all? Date night helped us remember all the reasons we fell in love while we were dating the first time, so—prepare for the cheesiness here—it was like falling in love all over again. *Cue *The Bachelor* theme music playing in the background.*

Jeff was immediately all in on my plan to dedicate a few hours to each other every week. In fact, we were soon sharing the responsibility of date night as we alternated planning and preparing the dates for each other. Over time, we were able to accumulate a year's worth of ideas that we can't wait to share with you. Before we jump in, here is a glimpse of what you can expect from these dates:

Won't Break the Bank

If you had an extra $20-$40 lying around, chances are you'd be hiring a babysitter and high-tailing it outta your house for date night. We hear you. The whole point of dating your spouse from your house is to save money, so we don't intend to blow your babysitter savings on pricey date night props or activities. All of these ideas promise to cost in the $0 - $15 range.

Perfect Backdrop to a Genuine Evening

As my husband and I started our dating journey, searching the internet for date ideas left us scrunching up our noses at a lot of over-the-top themed kits with unnecessary accessories, monthly subscription services, or over-sexualized dates that often felt forced. Our date plans are meant to be an easy backdrop for an evening to connect with each other in a genuine way.

Realistic and Accommodating Plans

As I said, we have kids. We have limited time and energy. Date night goes down when the kids do, so that only leaves a couple of precious hours to spend together. We have learned to simplify and get to the meat of the date in a realistic way. These ideas are easy to execute, utilize things you will likely already have, and can be adjusted to squeeze into any schedule.

Fave Fives

In the event that being confronted by a mass amount of date ideas all at one time overwhelms you, Jeff and I have each picked our five favorite dates to help you get started. Watch for the labels *Sarah's Fave Five* or *Jeff's Fave Five* to help you jump in with a no-fail date right out of the gate!

Share the Experience
One of my favorite things about date night is it gives Jeff and me more shared experiences, and my favorite thing about this book is that I get to see you share your experiences dating your spouse when you tag me on social media! We are on Facebook, Twitter, and Instagram (@housedates, #housedates). Find us, tag us, and let us share in your house dating journey!

Last Thing About the Last Thing
Take video clips and pictures of each date you do because there's a date idea at the end that will use all your dating snippets to create a digital scrapbook of your year of dating!

***

If you're ready, join me on a road where the limos transform into minivans, the mansion is the roof over your head, and the helicopter rides are largely powered by creativity. The good news is the only people who risk interrupting your one-on-one are the people who call you mom and dad, who, if all goes according to plan, are tucked away in bed. The best news is...your first date card is knocking!

BEING WITH YOU IS AS EASY AS PIE

Idea: Bake a pie together.

Plan: Hunt down your favorite pie recipe, or try a new one, and get baking! One person can do the crust while one works on the filling, or make the whole experience a combined effort. Get creative with the top of your pie by adding lattice or by carving your initials like we did. Whip out a game while your masterpiece cooks and then BAM! You've got yourselves a yummy treat to end the night!

Apple Pie

Crust
4 cups flour
1 ⅓ cup shortening
2 teaspoon salt
½ cup cold water

Apple Filling
6 tart apples - peeled, cored, and sliced
1/2 cup white sugar
2 teaspoons ground cinnamon
2 tablespoons all-purpose flour
3 tablespoons butter

Directions

1. Preheat oven to 350 degrees F (175 degrees C).
2. For the crust, mix the flour and salt. Cut in the shortening with a fork or pastry blender.
3. Add ice cold water to the dry ingredients until the dough sticks together when pinched. Do not add too much water or the dough will become tough.
4. Split the dough in half. Roll each each half of the dough on a lightly floured surface to create two 12-inch circles.
5. Place one of the dough circles in a lightly greased pie dish. Press the dough down gently so it is touching all surfaces of the dish. Trim the edges with a knife or kitchen scissors. Set the other circle aside.
6. Place sliced apples in a large bowl. In a small bowl combine sugar, cinnamon, and flour. Stir well and pour mixture over apples. Cut half of butter into small pieces and add to apples. Toss apples.
7. Pour apples into pastry-lined pie pan. Dot apples with the rest of the butter. Place second pastry circle on top. Seal edges and cut steam vents in top crust.
8. Bake in preheated oven for 45 to 55 minutes, until crust is golden brown.

---

https://www.allrecipes.com/recipe/15902/sundays-apple-pie

Will You Accept This Rose? This was the date that kicked off our year of in-house dating, so I made an intentional effort to treat it like a first date. With my phone hidden away for the night, I paid close attention to Jeff. I made an exaggerated effort to flirt like a second date was depending on it.

I even jokingly asked him questions one might ask on a first date thinking I already knew all of his answers. I was entertained when Jeff jumped into character and offered a few playful responses. At the end of the night, I sheepishly asked Jeff if he would date me again...and lucky for me (and you), he said yes!

A Night Under the Stars

Idea: Play a guessing game using quotes from your favorite TV shows.

Office-al First Texts: Jeff first visited my college apartment when my roommate, Leslie, invited him and a few other friends over to watch an episode of *The Office*. Mildly annoyed my apartment had become overpopulated against my will, I plopped on the couch, straining to hear over the rumble of intruders.

About halfway through the show, I began to notice Jeff across the room who was picking up on all the little things no one else seemed to catch. It became noticeable that our reactions to every joke were almost identical, causing us to eventually begin exchanging quick glances at each other after every punchline.

Jeff took my friendly eyes that evening as something to pursue. The next day I received a Michael Scott quote from someone my phone didn't recognize but my sense of humor did.

I shot back another quote without even needing to confirm it was Jeff. This quickly turned into a game of wits to see who could out-quote the other. The game lasted weeks with no clear winner, unless we're counting Jeff who won over my heart one hilarious text at a time.

Yes, a mockumentary brought Jeff and me together, and it continues to be one of our favorite shared interests. We reserve certain TV shows to watch together, we are constantly on the hunt for a new source of laughs, and we love to unwind with a few of our favorite characters. You do, too? I was hoping you'd say that.

Plan: Take some time to assemble quotes from your favorite TV shows and movies. Take turns guessing which character said which quote. You could say it's like *Name That Tune* but with quotes instead of lyrics and characters instead of song titles. Make it a theme by quoting under the stars with a bag of Starburst for an evening that's out of this world!

Production Help: To prevent overlap and to keep the quotes fresh for both of you, you could each choose which shows you'll be gathering quotes from.

For example, I found quotes from *The Office* and *Arrested Development* for Jeff to guess from, while I guessed from Jeff's assembly of *Mean Girls* and *Parks and Recreation* quotes. This way we weren't both sifting through quotes from the same show and spoiling the game.

You could also Google search "(Enter your favorite TV show) quotes" and then follow the most promising link. Print the page without reviewing its contents ahead of time. Then give alternating face-down pages to each of you so you can both guess from the same TV show.

Jump Into Love

Idea: Borrow the kids' trampoline for the night!
Jeff's Fave Five

Plan: I've found the quickest way to get your heart pounding for your spouse again: a trampoline! Dust off your front and back flips to show your spouse your most impressive tricks. We pulled out a camera and took pictures of each other while we were hopping around for some funny shots to remember the evening.

We spent some time with both of us on the trampoline for a few games of add-on–where one person does a trick and the next person has to do that trick plus one more, repeat, repeat, repeat until the person who can't remember the order owes the other one a kiss? On date night, you betcha!

Alternate Plan: If you don't have a trampoline, you could do hopscotch, jump rope, or even play add-on on stable ground!

Cool Down: I spent most of my teenage summer days out on the trampoline, either to get rid of extra energy, to indulge in some summer sunbathing, or just to get a minute to myself. Whenever my friends would come over, we'd run out to the trampoline as a private sanctuary to talk about whatever we wanted without having to worry about prodding parental ears.

As you might suspect, the teenage me was just as obsessed with dating and boys as the grown-up version of me, so that occupied much of the trampoline talk time.

I planned this date partially to see if the trampoline still held the magic it had when I was younger. Though I no longer had ample energy to burn off or time during the day to lie around soaking up the sun, I did suspect the trampoline might still offer itself as a sanctuary for Jeff and me to escape the prodding ears and demands of our...children.

Similar to my teenage jump sessions, Jeff and I began our trampoline time soaring through the air while we showed off our greatest tricks. As the night began winding down, our breaks between jumping stretched longer and longer until we finally succumbed to our tired legs.

We collapsed on our backs to look up at the stars and chat—like I did so frequently as a teenager. However, this time, my friend was my husband, and the boys we couldn't stop talking about and giggling over were the three sons we shared together. My life had come full (bouncy) circle in a way that was unexpectedly beautiful.

I wouldn't have guessed a night out on the trampoline with my husband would stir up tender, sentimental feelings and create such a special moment, but that's why you have to date your spouse. That's why you have to try new things together. There are magical moments hidden in ordinary things. You just might have to...jump through a few dates to find them.

YOU BRING COLOR TO MY WORLD

Idea: Color an adult coloring page.

Did I Cross the Line? If you peek behind the red, velvet curtain in the back corner of Walmart, you will find what's called "Adult Coloring Books." Now, don't be embarrassed. Anyone who sees you in there has the same fetish you do of finding the satisfaction they so desperately crave from the soft strokes...on a coloring book.

Fine. You guessed it. Walmart doesn't have a red curtain to mask the very much G-rated adult coloring books, but I still feel silly saying "adult coloring book" every time I happen to mention it.

A similarly uncomfortable feeling comes when I have to ask the librarian in the children's section where I can find "graphic novels" for my budding adolescent reader. Both of these things are nothing to be ashamed of, so let's all buck up together and admit to the world that we still sometimes like to color and look at cartoons, okay?!? Okay!!

Plan: Grab a coloring book. Any coloring book! They do have more complex versions for the ages-5-and-up crowd, or even better, print a few pages right off the internet after a simple (but perhaps carefully phrased) Google search of "Adult Coloring Pages." Take your pick from all the possibilities, and then color in the box next to "Plan Date Night" on your to-do list.

Theme: Make it a theme with a colorful treat. Pair your scribbling with some rainbow sorbet, Skittles, or Fruity Pebbles Treats. Recipe below!

"Adult" Fruity Pebbles Treats

3 tablespoons butter
1 10-ounce package of marshmallows
6 cups Fruity Pebbles cereal

Directions
Melt butter and marshmallows over medium heat until smooth. Remove from heat. Add Fruity Pebbles. Mix until evenly marshmallow-ed. Spread in a greased 9x13 cooking dish. Allow to cool. Or don't. Because you're an adult, and you can do what you want.

---

http://www.geniuskitchen.com/recipe/fruity-pebbles-treats-289757

I'm Beginning to Question Everything

Idea: Explore some conversation prompts.

Questionable Past: If you were to ask me to list my two most defining personality traits, I would tell you I'm a people pleaser and an introvert. Unfortunately for me, these traits do not often coexist in peaceful ways.

My opposing personality traits create a constant inner battle that became most apparent in the dating scene. Many of my first teenage dates were train wrecks of cringe-worthy small talk and anxious feet-shuffling as I hopelessly sputtered off pointless stories or attempted to make jokes my dates rarely perceived as funny.

When I could sense my date wasn't having a good time, the people-pleasing side of me would tense up and become overwhelmed by my inability to be the date my counterpart was hoping for. This realization would cause me to desperately continue talking nonsense while frantically eying my surroundings for a dark, quiet corner to find retreat.

Upon expressing these frustrations to my sister, she told me her secret. I chalk this up as the best dating (and possibly life) advice anyone has ever given me. Get your date to talk about himself. "Everyone loves talking about themselves," Becky casually revealed. "All you have to do is ask the right questions. If your date spends the whole night talking about himself, he'll think you're a great date, and he'll have a good time."

It worked. I found asking questions so much more approachable than being the source of entertainment. I learned how to dive into people's passions, uncover upbringings, and discover hidden interests.

Over time, I mastered the art of asking questions in the dating scene and outside of it. Asking questions perfectly allows me to mask my introvertedness (a cross between introversion and awkwardness) as I shine the spotlight on someone else, making that person feel good about our interaction while I get to sit back and enjoy an entertaining story or two.

My father-in-law calls me an interrogator. I've been (wrongly) labelled (by my grandma one time) the life of the party, and I've happily discovered the art of getting people to enjoy talking to me without having to do much of the talking.

Ask questions. Be interested. Get to the bottom of it. Dive into someone else's world. Focus on the person you're talking to instead of trying to get that person to focus on you. It's the secret to my success, and by success I mean my ability to lie low while still appearing to be sociable. And for a dark-closet-dwelling introvert, that's something.

(Stay tuned for my next book, *Introverts with Children: When Questions are No Longer the Answer*.)

Plan: You think you know everything there is to know about the person who shares a home with you...until you play this game and discover you know your spouse little more than you know the guy in front of you in line at McDonald's.

Each of you should come up with ten questions. Use a few of the questions below if you need a little help. You should both answer each set of questions and watch in amazement at all the new things you learn about the person you thought you knew everything about.

Production Help: Try these questions to get you started:

- What is one guilty pleasure you have that I don't know about?
- When was the last time you cried?
- What is your happiest childhood memory?
- Who was your first celebrity crush?
- What is one thing you refuse to share?
- If you could trade lives with anyone for a day, who would you choose and why?
- What is most likely to give you road rage?
- If you could go on an all-expenses paid trip tomorrow, where would you want to go?
- If you had to name a child tomorrow, what would you choose (one boy name and one girl name)?
- What is your favorite social media outlet?
- What is one habit you have that you would love to break?
- What is one TV show or movie you never get sick of?
- What is your favorite viral YouTube video?
- Describe your perfect sandwich.
- Tell me about a recurring dream you've had.
- Who was your favorite school teacher and why?

- Describe yourself in three words.
- If you knew you would succeed, what is one achievement you would like to accomplish?
- Tell me about your favorite scar.
- Has anyone ever saved your life?
- Who is your least favorite television character?
- What is something you are currently obsessed with?
- What candy bar/snack do you grab at a gas station on a road trip?
- What are three things you did every summer when you were a kid?
- What is one skill or quality of your mom and/or dad that you strive to possess?

I'm Falling Foooooore You

Idea: Play mini golf.
Sarah's Fave Five

Plan: I often found myself suffering from date nighter's block in the middle of winter when snow prevented us from venturing outside. Date night after date night was not only repeatedly restricted to the inside of our house, but was also pinned down to the same lowly living room.

Enter mini golf. If you have a golfer in the family (or maybe a friendly neighbor with some clubs), grab a couple of putters and get to work creating your own mini golf course to liven up your living room!

Production Help: We used books, DVD cases, toys, and pillows for "bunkers." Anything and everything in your house is now a tool to morph your space into a resourceful course.

Due to limited space, we created our golf course hole by hole. We'd set up the obstacles, play it, destroy it, and make the next. Finish off the night with donuts (you know, hole-in-one?), or by watching a golf movie like *Happy Gilmore* or *The Greatest Game Ever Played*.

It's a PAR-TEE: I loved this idea because as we started I was worried we would become unenthusiastic and disinterested with each new hole we had to construct throughout the game. When we got into it, that actually turned out to be our favorite part!

The more we played, the more our house took on the role of a 5-star golf course offering increasingly abundant variations of believable bunkers, makeshift water obstacles, or stand-in sand traps. We got better at course building as the game went on, helping our date stay happily "on course."

Let's See How This Shakes Out

Idea: Make ice cream in a bag.

Plan: Did you know with three simple ingredients and a little bit of an arm workout, you can make ice cream? You heard me right. You don't need no stinkin' machine.

Gather ½ cup of half and half, 1 tablespoon of sugar, and ¼ teaspoon of vanilla. Throw that in a pint-sized Ziploc bag (I have doubled or tripled with good results, both in the taste of the ice cream and in the definition of my biceps). Throw the pint-sized bag into a gallon-sized bag with a good amount of ice and salt, then start shaking.

After about 10-15 minutes, your milk will be sufficiently shaken and will begin to take the form of your favorite frozen treat. Pile on some toppings and dig in! Psst...here's a secret: this treat is basically guiltless because you likely will have burned off all the calories contained in the snack throughout your laborious milk churning!

Theme It! Now that your muscles are warmed up, they're ready for a game of Yahtzee! You could also opt to continue your shaking with an impromptu dance session in the living room, or maybe you prefer to appreciate someone else's dance moves with a dancing movie like *Step Up*, *Grease*, or an episode of *So You Think You Can Dance*.

I Hope We Cross Paths Tonight

Idea: Play travel magazine games.

I'd Die For You: Do you ever look back on your life and wonder how you didn't get murdered? After reflecting on some of my uninhibited life choices, it has become clear that somebody is really looking out for me.

For example, one time this guy I barely knew asked me out on a date. When I got in his car, he told me he was taking me to our college's "tunnels." "Oooohh. That sounds fun," I said, my only concern being whether or not my batting eyelashes were on pointe.

So then the creep takes me to the school, pulls out this special set of keys that, looking back, should have been flagged as highly suspicious. However, I was 19, naive, and nothing but impressed.

As the once-secured door opened, I walked into a ginormous, vacant, underground tube. Naturally, I giddily and without question closed the door behind me, locking me in what could have been the perfect crime scene of the perfect murder.

Thankfully Jeff isn't a murderer. And his only intention was to impress me with his unrestrained accessibility to underground, once-thought-to-be-only-mythical pathways. And it worked. It worked so well that he even got me to go to his place afterwards.

Still riding the high of escaping my chance to be the next victim featured on *20/20*, Jeff wooed me once again when he whipped out a travel magazine instead of a gun so we could have a Sudoku face-off.

I guess that's the secret of finding love. Give someone the opportunity to murder you several times in one night, and if they don't, you'll probably live a long and happy life together. Worked for me, anyway.

Plan: Pick up a travel puzzle magazine from the store, or find some online to print. Try crossword puzzles, word searches, or Sudoku. Print off two of the same one and have a battle, or put your brains together to find the answers. Bonus points if you both make it out of the night alive!

Namaste With You

Idea: Complete a yoga workout together.

Plan: Let's give a big shout-out to YouTube for giving us free access to all the yoga instructors we could never afford. Work those limbs with your spouse! You can take it light and easy, or go for a full-body burn. You could even try couples yoga which includes poses meant for two people to do together.

Production Help: Here are yoga options from some of my favorite YouTube workout channels:

PopSugar Fitness: 30-Minute Yoga With Adriene to Reduce Stress. https://www.youtube.com/watch?v=q2G5ZX0JgvQ

Fitness Blender: Refresh and Restore: Stretching, Pilates, Yoga Workout for Tight Muscles. https://www.youtube.com/watch?v=Pp8UNgkcAYs

Dutch Smiling Yogi: Partner Yoga Class for Beginners (Free, Full Class). https://www.youtube.com/watch?v=j0HGMmrdUco

Cool Down: After all that work, you deserve a treat! Cool down with a strawberry yogurt smoothie to make you a yogi both inside and out!

Yogi Smoothie

8 strawberries
½ cup milk
½ cup plain yogurt
3 tablespoons sugar
2 teaspoons vanilla extract
6 ice cubes, crushed

Directions

Add all the ingredients except for the ice into a blender. Once mixed, toss in the ice. Mix again until creamy and...smooth!

---

https://www.allrecipes.com/recipe/20792/b-and-ls-strawberry-smoothie

You Are My Bucket List

Idea: Write a bucket list.
Great for New Year's!

I Want to Share My Life (List) with You: Senior year of high school had me in an Honors English class where my teacher, as a way to force our adolescent minds to momentarily think about our futures, required each student to create a "Life List" of 100 things we hoped to accomplish before we die.

I grew to love my life list. In fact, I loved it so much that as Jeff and I began dating, I slyly challenged him to create his own life list. The sly part was that I did this right before I left for Christmas break as a subtle way to get him to think of me while I was away.

My plan proved to be successful when I got an email a few days later with his list. I loved reading over his life vision, especially when I got to "100: Spend New Year's Eve with Sarah Thomas."

His flirtatious life list prompted me to dutifully travel four hours just to spend New Year's Eve with him—only to find myself from the hours of 11:45 PM to 12:15 AM huddled in a corner on the floor by myself while he ended up on a loveseat rekindling a bromance with a good friend from years' past. It was a confusing time for all of us.

We worked through it though. And *Spoiler Alert* he did finally kiss me (way too many weeks later).

Plan: Write a life list. Do it the Honors English way and come up with 100 things you would like to say you've done by the time you're on your deathbed. We were encouraged to write things that seemed impossible, to involve our passions, to include big goals and little goals, places to travel, experiences to try, foods to taste, things to become, titles to hold, possessions to own, anything!

I remember my teacher encouraging us to write anything that came to mind because it's so neat to see the seemingly impossible or insignificant things come about. Let loose and embrace every little desire that emerges. Then start living and see where life takes you!

Your Life, Abridged: Maybe you don't want to shoot for a whole life list. Try a short-term bucket list. For example, we love to sit down at the beginning of each summer and write down all the activities we hope to do for the next three months of sunshine.

We make a big poster out of it and check things off as we get them done. It gives us something to look forward to and a sense of accomplishment as we look back on the variety of fun things we were able to do once the season is over.

You're a Great Catch

Idea: Head outside to play catch.
Jeff's Fave Five

Be an All-Star: Jeff planned this date for us and knocked it out of the park when he surprised me with a "ticket" Friday morning before he left for work. He found a baseball ticket template online and entered in the date and time of our big game as my invitation to the evening.

Jeff came home from work with all the baseball food he could find at the grocery store to make the evening feel like an authentic night at the ballpark–landing this date in his Fave Five.

Plan: Round up a baseball (or any ball) and find a patch of grass (or some open space in the living room) to toss the ball back and forth to each other.

Production Help: If it's summer, you could get wild by adding water balloons into the mix. Perfect your overhand by backing up with each toss. See how many times you can throw to each other without dropping the ball. Head inside for a baseball movie like *Fever Pitch*, *The Sandlot*, or Jeff's favorite: *The Natural*.

If you're really committed, you could even pace around the couch during the movie with a tray full of hot dogs and Cracker Jacks. No matter how you choose to play out this date, it's sure to be a home run!

I'm Quite Fondue of You

Idea: Dip food in chocolate or cheese.

Plan: Throw some quick ingredients into a slow cooker, or over the stove, or heck, even pop them in the microwave for a fondue night! Bonus points if you actually have a fondue fountain. Try my favorite chocolate fondue recipe listed below, or find a cheese variation.

Load up on a bunch of dippers and light some candles for ambience. You might discover like we did that your candle flame can easily become multi-functional when you use it to roast a few marshmallows to make s'mores as you're dipping.

Production Help: Try this chocolate fondue recipe from melskitchencafe.com:

Perfect Chocolate Fondue

10 ounces semisweet or bittersweet chocolate

1/3 cup milk

1/3 cup heavy cream

1 teaspoon vanilla extract

Lots of dipping options (strawberries, bananas, small Rice Krispies squares, vanilla cookies, marshmallows, graham crackers, etc.)

Directions

1. In a saucepan, combine the chocolate, milk, and cream and heat on low, stirring often, until the chocolate is completely melted and the mixture is smooth. Don't let it come to a boil; keep it on low heat.
2. Once melted, stir in the vanilla extract. If needed, stir in heavy cream or milk a tablespoon at a time to adjust for a thinner consistency. Pour the mixture into a fondue pot or small slow cooker to keep warm while serving.

---

https://www.melskitchencafe.com/perfect-chocolate-fondue

Let's Skip Town

Idea: Plan a vacation.

The At-Home Slump: Listen up. You know I think you're financially savvy and romantically chic for dating your spouse from your house, but every once in a while I completely understand that you might be feeling a little frustrated to be repeatedly stuck at home on a Friday night while all of your single, rich, and/or exotic friends (you know the ones) are Facebook updating you of their endless, highly-adventurous and highly-enviable travels.

I get that this could cause you to reflect on what has become of your life as you slink further into your recliner with a bag of powdered Donettes while you unfairly decide your life is a stew of dull as you face the harsh reality that you've got nothing more than dentist appointments to look forward to on the calendar.

Plan: This date card couldn't have come at a better time. Let's liven things up! While you may be trapped in your house this Friday night, use this time to plan a vacation for later on. Whether it be a semi-planned vacation for this year or a bucket list trip for the distant future, plan out the details!

Talk about what you'd like to do while you're there, where you could stay, what food you'll have to try, and how much you'll need to save. Set a goal and make a plan to turn your travel dreams into reality!

It might be "window vacationing" for now (think window shopping, but for a vacation), but without a plan, no vacation will ever happen. Get something on the calendar to look forward to, work towards, and have a ton of fun planning and fantasizing about it in the meantime!

Join the Club

Idea: Have a book club with your spouse.

Plan: You know that episode of *The Office* where Pam, Oscar, and Toby have an elite and exclusive book club? Consider that the inspiration for this idea. You and your spouse are now members of The Finer Things Club. You could even pretend your kids are envious coworkers who wish they could join but are not refined enough.

Pick a book one of you loves and the other hasn't read or a book you are both interested in reading that neither of you has read. Spend a few weeks doing your date night homework by reading the book. Meet together on date night to discuss (teacups, costumes, and themed music optional).

Book Suggestions:

- *The 5 Love Languages* by Gary Chapman
- *The Seven Principles of Making Marriage Work* by John M. Gottman
- *The Boys in the Boat* by Daniel James Brown
- *How to Win Friends and Influence People* by Dale Carnegie
- *The 7 Habits of Highly Effective People* by Stephen Covey
- *Five Days at Memorial* by Sheri Fink
- *The Princess Bride* by William Goldman
- *The Alchemist* by Paulo Coelho

Pucker Up!

Idea: Make lemonade with your main squeeze.

First Kiss, No Joke: Before you can take another date idea from me seriously, I think I need to "smack" some credentials on the table. In a book about love, the best credentials I can offer are the makings of our love story, which I can sense you're aching to know more about.

What better place to start than with our first kiss? What's that, Jeff? Oh yes. There are much better places to start than our first kiss because it took Jeff approximately 2.5 million dates before he mustered up the courage to lay one on me. And, by the way, he only laid one on me because I essentially begged him to. Let's jump to the scene:

We were at his parents' house to watch a movie in their basement. We had been friends for a few months and had been on several dates, but we still had not so much as held the other's hand. I sat on the couch first with my left hand conveniently accessible. Jeff got the movie going and then sat next to me perfectly placing his hand into mine on the way down.

I had a hard time keeping cool as I tried to mask my excitement through the rest of the movie. As a habitual over-thinker, I spent the next two hours discreetly staring at our hands and what this meant for our relationship.

Did he mean to put his hand in mine or was it an accident that he's now committed to? I questioned. *Is he going to try to kiss me tonight?* I took bashful peeks up at his eyes to try to get a read on his intentions. *Oh my gosh, are we boyfriend and girlfriend?* I thought between nearly-hyperventilative breaths.

I began to irrationally escalate the situation throughout the whole movie. The longer our debatably accidental handhold remained in place, the more convinced I was that Jeff Excell was my insta-boyfriend. (Had memes been a thing back then, I would have been the face of the Overly Attached Girlfriend.)

The movie ended. My eyes bugged in nervous anticipation. The next step was obvious. Now that Jeff was my assumed boyfriend, we had to kiss. I expectantly looked up at him. He coyly looked down at me. And there we sat.

My overthinking kicked into high gear as I willed him to kiss me while simultaneously throwing myself into a fit of self-consciousness as I wondered why he wasn't seizing the opportunity. I mean, only two hours into becoming hypothetical boyfriend/girlfriend, and he wasn't even kissing me? Did we need couples counseling?

Suddenly a joke I had once heard popped into my mind, so I broke the silence with a timid, "Knock, knock."

"Who's there?" Jeff said with a laugh.

"Kiss," I said, waiting for him to foresee the end of my joke.

He played along, "Kiss who?"

With a surprisingly cool delivery I answered, "Me."

He took the hint, and we dodged that visit to couples counseling two hours into our relationship. And yeah, we did make my delusions a reality that same night as we decided to make our coupledom official.

And yes, you caught that right. We held hands, kissed, and became boyfriend/girlfriend all in the same night. I told you we had credentials.

Plan: This date will have you puckering up faster than you can tell a corny joke in your parents' basement. I'm talking lemonade, and I'm talking freshly squeezed.

Kick the Kool-Aid to the curb and whip up a drink that will give you credentials...credentials to work for Chick-Fil-A as their go-to lemonade specialist. This one is great for the summer when you can sip your squeezed drink in the backyard as you retell (and relive? *wink, wink*) your first kiss story.

Love-ly Lemonade

1 ¾ cups white sugar
1 ½ cups lemon juice
8 cups water

Directions

1. In a small saucepan combine sugar and 1 cup water. Bring to boil and stir to dissolve sugar. Allow to cool to room temperature, then cover and refrigerate until chilled.
2. Remove seeds from lemon juice but leave pulp. In pitcher, stir together chilled syrup, lemon juice, and remaining 7 cups water.
3. Optional: Mix in some fresh strawberries, raspberries, or peach juice for a lemonade-sampling extravaganza!

---

https://www.allrecipes.com/recipe/32385/best-lemonade-ever/

You Always Cheer Me Up

Idea: Create a family cheer and mission statement.

Back to My Root, Root, Roots: I don't know what prompted it, and I couldn't tell you what events led to its creation, but my family had a cheer growing up. This cheer wasn't something we reserved for sporting events or special occasions. It was chanted every Monday night to close our weekly "family night." Oh, you want to hear it? I thought you might say that.

"We are the BEST! We stand the TEST! In us you trust—the FAMILY THOMAS!"

Cute, right? I knew you'd warm up to the idea. For me, one of the most unsettling things about growing up was discovering family cheers were not a mandatory part of every family unit. I grew to accept that we were a cheerful anomaly and went about my adult life clutching the memories of my weekly pep rally whenever I needed a pick-me-up.

Eventually I found myself two kids into growing my family and in obvious need of a morale boost. I felt like our family needed something to stand for, something we could all get behind, and a common rally that would bring us all together. I knew what needed to be done.

After the kids were in bed one night, Jeff and I bounced ideas off each other until we came up with our very own family cheer:

46

"E-X-C-E-Double-L! We're kind and smart and really swell. We are the fam-ily Excell!"

We practiced it a few times and then realized it sounded like we were saying, "We're kind of smart and really swell," so we did some quick editing until we got the finished product:

"E-X-C-E-Double-L! We're SMART and KIND and really SWELL! We are the fam-ily EXCELL!"

You wouldn't believe how much more we smile and high kick now. It's life changing.

Plan: Create a family cheer! Come up with a quick, catchy summary of what you want your family to stand for. Why are you awesome? What do you love about you? Who do you want to become? What would you want your kids chanting to themselves? Once you have the words in place, you could even come up with hand motions and footwork, or you could expand your cheer into a family mission statement.

An Effective Date Night: In his book, *The 7 Habits of Highly Effective People*, Stephen Covey encourages families to come up with a mission statement. He explains that to be more effective with your life you need to have end goals in sight, and then create a plan to get there.

Covey says on his website, "Develop a personal mission statement. It focuses on what you want to be and do. It is your plan for success. It reaffirms who you are, puts your goals in focus, and moves your ideas into the real world.

Your mission statement makes you the leader of your own life. You create your own destiny and secure the future you envision."

Take a minute to think about what you want your family to look like in 5, 10, 15, 20, 50 years. What values will your family need to have to get to where you hope you will be? What will your family stand for? What is important to you? What will lead to your successes? Write it down, tweak it, think about it, and spend some time sharing your family vision with each other.

Covey, Stephen. "Habit 2: Begin With End In Mind."
FranklinCovey,
www.franklincovey.com/the-7-habits/habit-2.html.

LOVE IS A BATTLEFIELD

Idea: Build a fort together.
Jeff's Fave Five

Plan: If love is a battlefield, you're going to need a good hideout. Pull out the extra sheets, yank off the couch cushions, drag the dining room chairs into the living room, and build yourselves a fort your childhood would be proud of. Once the fort is in place and as secure as a blanket fort can be, enjoy your hideout by watching a movie, eating a treat, or playing a game inside.

Production Help: Make it a battlefield theme by playing the card game War in your fort. You could also play Battleship by each drawing two 10 x 10 squares, one labeled "My Ships" and the other labeled "Enemy Ships":

- Plot all of your ships by coloring connecting blocks on the grid according to its size. Each player will color in 5 blocks for an aircraft carrier, 4 blocks for a battleship, 3 blocks for a cruiser, 2 blocks for a patrol boat, and 3 blocks for a submarine. Ships may not overlap.

- Take turns firing upon the enemy by calling out plot points, for example, A-5. Mark your shot as a hit (X) or a miss (O) on your enemy ship grid according to your opponent's reply.

- When your enemy fires upon you, answer hit or miss, according to your enemy's shot. Mark your hit ships with an X on the "My Ships" grid.

- When the ships are sunk, you must inform your opponent that it is sunk and which ship it is.

- The first person to sink all of the enemy ships wins the game.

Hidden Talents: I suspected Jeff would enjoy this date, but I underestimated his interest in constructing blankets into a glorified tent. Right after I told Jeff the date plan our baby started crying, so I ran up to his room to calm him down. In the five minutes I was gone, Jeff had managed to gather every conceivable fort-building material from around the house and was already starting to troubleshoot design ideas. He turned our entire living room into a blanket mansion as we taught each other all the fort-building tricks of our younger years.

---

https://www.kidspot.com.au/things-to-do/activity-articles/how-to-play-battleships/news-story

We Are Two Peas In a Pod

Idea: Listen to a podcast together.

Learning to Share: If you were to ask me, the most beneficial part of date night is that it offers you and your spouse a new shared experience. There are some weeks Jeff and I are so busy it feels like we barely say more to each other than, "Hey, have you changed the baby's diaper yet?" Shared experiences are what help us remember we have things in common besides the miniature housemates who share our genes.

One of my favorite podcasts to listen to is *Reply All*, a show about weird things that have happened because of the internet. Episode 116 discussed an NBA basketball player nicknamed "The Process" who was featured for his hilarious tweets, but the show basically had to uncover the sports star's entire life story to help listeners understand his humor.

As a sports un-enthusiast, I suddenly had a vast amount of knowledge I didn't quite know what to do with about an obscure sports figure. One evening I was sitting with Jeff, a knowledgeable sports guy, when I decided to "throw him a curve ball" (translate that into basketball).

I managed to nonchalantly work "The Process" into our evening conversation for the sole purpose of seeing Jeff's confusion, surprise, and general elation that I was "taking a swing" at understanding one of his previously ignored interests.

Jeff's reaction to my sports talk was to be expected. What was unexpected was that I actually enjoyed talking sports with him! It was a topic we had never dabbled in together, yet there we were 20 minutes into a conversation about some basketball player who I now know more than I ever thought I would want to know about, and our conversation was actually coherent.

Every time Jeff and I try something new together it reignites all the feelings we had when we were first getting to know each other because it opens up the chance to get to know new parts about each other that are still waiting to be explored.

Plan: Agree upon a podcast to listen to. You can either spend the evening listening to it together or listen to several episodes ahead of time and spend the evening discussing thoughts, ideas, and stories the podcast brings to your attention. Use it as a stepping stone to learn more about how your spouse sees things. And then maybe go eat some peas just for the sake of sticking with a theme.

Production Help: Here are a few of my favorite thought-provoking podcasts to get you started:

RadioLab
Serial
Reply All
Where Should We Begin?

Revisionist History
By the Book
More Perfect
The Habitat

It's Time for an Up-Date!

Idea: Complete a house project together.

Big Gaines: The worst part about watching the show *Fixer Upper* is not only does it make you realize how many updates your house could use, but it also brings to your attention the palpable marital happiness of Chip and Joanna Gaines.

Ten minutes into my first time ever watching the show left me feeling like both my house and my relationship needed a total makeover, causing me to urgently scream at Jeff across our out-of-date living space, "HONEY, WE'RE SHIPLAPPING THE WHOLE HOUSE TONIGHT!"

Now, now. I can hear some of you saying, "A house project is going to improve my relationship with my spouse? That's more like a relationship wrecking ball!" My husband would probably agree with you. He is quick to grumble any time I try to disguise my to-do list as a date idea.

However, house projects are one of my favorite things to do with Jeff! Once we are in the thick of a project, I love working with him towards a common goal. I love the creativity of transforming our living space into something fresh and new, and I love the accomplishment we feel together after we've finished a project. Grab a paintbrush and get fixer uppering!

Plan: Tackle a house project that you've been meaning to get done but haven't found the time. Spruce up your house by planting a few flowers in the garden, painting a wall, adding photos to empty frames, rearranging furniture, adding a backsplash to your kitchen, hanging curtains for your windows, adding hardware to bare cabinets, renovating an old piece of furniture, adding shelves to a wall, or simply organizing a messy closet. Find something you both agree could use some work and get busy!

How Do I Love Thee?
Let Me Count the Ways.

Idea: Complete a paint-by-numbers.

Procrasti-date: It was in desperation one Friday morning that I scoured the shelves of Walmart in search of some last-minute date night inspiration. I owe this successful idea to aisle 9–the craft section–where a paint-by-numbers kit practically poltergeisted off the shelf shouting, "I will make your date night dreams come true!"

Or maybe I'm the one who screamed while lunging at the set, but either way, I suddenly had the perfect activity to help us unwind after a busy week.

Plan: If your world is a tornado of chaos (think kids), you may find serenity in taking a black and white pattern and filling it with predetermined colors. Perfectly placed shading is exactly what you never realized you needed to feel like your life once again has order.

Pick up a paint-by-numbers kit at Walmart (around $7.00), or if you already have paint and paintbrushes, you can print your canvas right off the internet. Search Google Images for "paint-by-numbers" and the options are limitless!

Production Help: Release your creativity with a wave of classical music that will make you feel like world-class artists. Get fancy with some sparkling cider. Not only will this activity provide you with a minimum of three hours' worth of date night entertainment, but it can also double as sentimental artwork to display in your house for the next 50+ years! I know. I was shocked by the versatility of this idea, too.

Calling All the Numbers Guys! My husband was working as an accountant when I revealed this date idea to him. As one who had never considered himself much of an artist, he was skeptical to spend the evening with a paintbrush in hand.

However, as soon as we got going, he found this was exactly the kind of painting for him. Assigning colors to numbers and filling in clearly-defined areas were two things he could wrap his number-crunching brain around. This date has the power to make even the right-brained people feel creative, dubbing it a favorite for all.

History...or Her Story?

Idea: Share memories from when you were dating.
Sarah's Fave Five

History Lesson: One of my dad's more inspired moments of life happened when he was talking with a married couple who had slowly begun to notice nothing but each other's faults. They came to my dad looking for advice on how to mend their marriage.

My dad simply asked them to tell him about their first interactions with each other. As the couple reminisced about the times they found each other enticing, endearing, and irresistible, they were reminded of why they fell in love. Rekindling those feelings helped them make steps towards cherishing each other like they did when they first met.

Plan: Take an evening to reminisce with your spouse about all your first encounters. Write down your favorite stories from both of your perspectives and then come together to see how they're the same and how they differ. It would also be fun to videotape some of your favorite first memories together as a unique way to capture your history for your kids and grandkids to enjoy!

Pop Quiz: Here are some questions to get you going:

- **First Impressions:** Where did you first see each other? How did you meet? Do you remember what you said? Did you like each other right away? What drew you to each other?
- **First Date:** Who asked whom out? Where did you go? What memorable or funny things happened? Did you kiss? Did you immediately want to go out again? Can you

remember anything specific the other person said? Do you remember what you were each wearing?

- **The Little Things:** What was it that enticed you about your spouse? What personality traits did you find charming? What physical feature were you most drawn to? What did you initially admire about your spouse? How was your spouse different than other people you had dated?

- **The Moment You Knew:** Talk about the moment you knew the other person was for you. What were you doing? When did it hit you?

- **Most Fun Date:** What was one of your favorite dates before you were married? What made it fun? What did you talk about? What stood out to you about your spouse on that date?

- **Catastrophic Date:** Did any dates not go as planned? Were you able to laugh through it? Did anything unexpected happen? How did each of you handle the situation?

- **Meeting the Parents:** How did you feel when it was time to meet the parents/family? Do you remember what you talked about with them? Did you say anything embarrassing?

- **Proposal:** Share your proposal story! What was the most magical part? Did everything go as it was supposed to? Did you both know the proposal was coming or was it a complete surprise? Did she help pick out the ring?

- **Wedding:** What funny memories do you have from your wedding? Who was more nervous? Did everything go according to plan? Which wedding guests were the most memorable? Which gift did you enjoy the most?

Date Night with a Twist

Idea: Play Twister!

Plan: The twist is...Twister! Raid your parents' basement for your favorite board...er...mat game and set it up for a fun test of flexibility and agility with your spouse.

In order to keep both players in the game, we flicked the spinner ahead of time for about fifteen turns' worth and then wrote down on a piece of paper what each progressive move would be. There's probably an app for that nowadays, but take it old school with the pen and paper if you have to!

Make it a Theme! Once you're all twisted out, you can either make big, fluffy, the-kind-you-find-at-the-mall pretzels like we did, or you could keep it easy with chocolate covered pretzels or Twizzlers. Top the night off with the movie *Twister* if you're looking to wring out as much twisting as you can from the night.

Chewy Soft Pretzels

Dough

2 1/2 cups (10 1/2 ounces) all-purpose flour
1/2 teaspoon salt
1 teaspoon sugar
2 1/4 teaspoons instant yeast
1 cup (8 ounces) very warm water

Topping

1/2 cup (4 ounces) warm water
2 tablespoons baking soda
Coarse salt (optional)
3 tablespoons butter, melted

Directions

1. In a large bowl or the bowl of an electric mixer, place the flour, salt, sugar and yeast. Mix to just combine. Add the water and mix well, adding more flour, as needed, a bit at a time to form a soft, smooth dough that clears the sides and bottom of the bowl.

2. Knead the dough, by hand or machine, for about 5 minutes, until it is soft, smooth and quite slack. The goal is to get a really soft dough that isn't overly sticky. Lightly flour the dough and place it in a plastic bag; close the bag, leaving room for the dough to expand, and let it rest for 30 minutes or up to 60 minutes.

3. Preheat your oven to 500°F. Prepare two baking sheets by lining them with parchment paper.

4. Transfer the dough to a lightly greased work surface, and divide it into eight equal pieces. Allow the pieces to rest, uncovered, for 5 minutes. While the dough is resting, combine the 1/2 cup warm water and the baking soda, and place it in a shallow bowl or pie plate. Make sure the baking soda is thoroughly dissolved.

5. Roll each piece of dough into a long, thin rope (anywhere from 14 to 22 inches long), and twist each rope into a

pretzel. Dip each pretzel in the baking soda wash (this will give the pretzels a nice, golden-brown color), and place them on the baking sheets. Sprinkle them lightly with coarse, kosher, or pretzel salt. Allow them to rest, uncovered, for 10 minutes.

6. Bake the pretzels for 7 to 9 minutes or until they're golden brown. Bake one sheet at a time—it won't hurt the other pretzels to chill out for a little longer.

7. Remove the pretzels from the oven, and brush them thoroughly with melted butter. Keep brushing the butter until you've used it all up; it may seem like a lot, but that's what gives these pretzels their ethereal taste. Eat the pretzels warm, or reheat them in the microwave or oven.

---

https://www.melskitchencafe.com/chewy-soft-pretzels/

A Night at the Theater

Idea: Get cozy with a movie.

Plan: Movie night is always a favorite after a busy week. Call your home TV a movie screen, and just like that you've changed your humble living room into a movie theater! While I try to make date night a little more interactive than plopping down for a movie, every once in awhile it's nice to cuddle up, grab some treats, and veg out together.

Production Help: To make the night special, have a few things ready ahead of time to show the date was thought out and intentional. Step up your mundane movie game by snagging some movie-theater-style boxed candy from the store along with a mandatory bag of popcorn.

You may want to pick up a Redbox to treat yourselves to a movie you haven't seen yet. Feel free to use the evening as an excuse to snuggle like you did back when you were dating the first time around.

Let Your Spouse Steal the Show: I didn't find out until I was in too deep that my husband is a huge *Lord of the Rings* fan. As a girl who was always more into things like...ahem...*The Bachelor*, *Lord of the Rings* wasn't ever something that caught my interest.

To show my husband my love and devotion to him, I offered a date night where we watched his favorite movie, so I could gain a deeper appreciation for an interest he had. While I feel like movie watching can often be a throw-away date, this added meaning to our night.

Go ahead and sit down with your spouse's favorite movie. Figure out what they love about it, and you might find it uncovers something new and endearing to love about your spouse...like their obsession with gremlins.

Join Me For A Liqui-Date

Idea: Find items around your house to sell.

Hard Sell: If you learn nothing else from this book, learn that when you have a new baby, he/she does not automatically get added onto your health insurance just for being in your family. Allegedly there's a *enter sassy air quotes* "30-day" "window" for adding your baby to your plan.

If you get baby added so much as one day past the *more dramatic air quotes* "nationally" "recognized" "enrollment" "window," you will suddenly find yourself with a $750 doctor's bill for three vaccinations at a thought-it-was-covered-and-completely-free doctor's appointment.

Let me tell you, very few people in the billing department will offer their condolences upon hearing the sob story of your tragically blonde moment which led to the first year of your child's life being uninsured.

What do you do for date night when you're suddenly $750 in the red? You sell. And you sell fast. You run around the house and assess your assets and quickly decide that everything must go. You start to notice all the things hanging around that you never use. It's time to assign a price tag, and send it packing.

After saying goodbye to a barely-used archery bow, a set of handmade curtains, and a garage sale's worth of items, we finally gathered enough money to stick a Band-Aid on our unexpected expenses, though our ego was still bruised. We found it was refreshing to clear some of our old junk out of our apartment. It was fun to price things out together, it was thrilling to make a sale, and it was rewarding to come up with the money we owed in a cleansing way.

Plan: You don't have to have your finances dip into the red to try this date idea! The better option is to use this idea to earn a little babysitter money or to have some extra cash to put down on a new purchase.

For example, we bought new dining room chairs and almost took our old ones to the dump before thinking, *Hey, maybe someone would buy these*. One hour on Facebook Marketplace and they sold for $40!

Go around your house reminding yourselves that one man's trash is another man's treasure. Look at your belongings and decide what you could do without: unused wedding gifts, forgotten hobbies, appliances you're ready to upgrade.

Throw each individual item up on Facebook Marketplace for a quick and easy sell, or if you have enough items, price them and hold a yard sale over the weekend. You'll love the feeling of making money while you're decluttering!

You're the Apple of My Eye

Idea: Dip apples in caramel for a festive fall date.

Plan: If leaves are dropping and pumpkin spice is in the air, I know you're going to be in the mood to dunk a bushel of apples into a giant pot of caramel.

We used popsicle sticks to spear apples and then went hog-wild dipping and drizzling a once-healthy snack into an indulgent ball of fall fantasies. My fall fantasies are heavily reliant on food. Dipped in caramel. Yours too? Then get dipping, my friend.

Production Help: In the baking section of the grocery store, you can find Kraft Caramel Bits. They're little pieces of easily-meltable caramel that make dipping a breeze. After a coat of caramel, drizzle white or milk chocolate over your apples for visual appeal. Try crushed peanuts or sprinkles to instantly make your treat gourmet.

Now You're Speaking My Language

Idea: Discover and discuss your love languages.
Sarah's Fave Five

Plan: Do you ever look at your spouse and think, *Do we even speak the same language?!?* If we're talking about love languages, the answer is probably no. Gary Chapman's book *The 5 Love Languages* is just the eye-opener your marriage needs to learn how to connect with your spouse on his or her level. It will change the way you view all of your interactions with your spouse!

You don't even have to commit to the book to get a diagnosis on which languages represent love for you. There's a quick online quiz where you can discover your love languages and then you can compare and contrast with your spouse!

Mi Amor: Spanish may not be one of the five languages Chapman refers to, but words of affirmation, quality time, receiving gifts, acts of service, and physical touch are. Use these questions to learn more about your language!

- Tell me an example of when I spoke one of your love languages in a way that translated.
- Tell me specifically of a time I didn't quite speak your language and could have done better.
- Share a specific time you were trying to express love and felt it wasn't understood.

- Share your parents' and family's love languages to better understand how you each "learned to speak" love growing up.
- What will you do differently now that you better understand how to show love to your partner?
- What is something you will appreciate more about your spouse now that you know it's an expression of his/her love?

Filling Up the Love Tank: I have come to notice my love languages developed through the way my family interacted with each other growing up. In my family, the way we spoke our love was through acts of service. An emptied dishwasher, a mowed lawn, or a made bed were the ways we showed we cared. Along with that was an unspoken rule that whenever you drove someone else's car, even if it was only to go half a mile down the road, you were expected to fill their car up with gas.

To me this was so obvious. Filling the tank was a way to say thanks for the borrowed car. It showed you cared to leave the car in better shape than you found it. It was courteous to make sure you didn't put someone out by using all of their gas. There were millions of hidden meanings beneath a full tank of gas that I grew to believe were across-the-board understandings.

Unfortunately for Jeff, he did not have the same unspoken truths regarding gasoline gauges. One day after Jeff had used my car, I excitedly hopped in the driver's seat expecting to see my once half-full tank now reading full. Instead, I watched in horror as the needle trembled to a halt right above the quarter-tank marker.

I cursed Jeff's name all the way to the gas station. I had to do the job that was meant to be done by him just to spite him (even though had I been the last to drive the car, I wouldn't have been filling up the gas so soon). Then I had to charge back into our house to passive aggressively stare at Jeff until he noticed my quiet surges of rage.

When he finally asked me what was wrong, I sternly explained my stance. With each attempted explanation that gas equals love and empty tank equals does not care, I heard myself blubbering a list of unfair expectations. As a last attempt to gather my thoughts, I finally summarized with, "Filling up someone's gas tank is like telling them, 'I love you!'" And that's when I knew I was wrong. I wasn't wrong for thinking a full tank of gas means "I love you" to me, but I was wrong for expecting Jeff to know that without any previous knowledge of my family's obsession with acts of service.

Jeff has since filled up my gas tank every time he drives my car. Because now he knows. And now it means even more to me because I know he's doing it because he knows it's important to me. To tie it all together, Gary Chapman's book actually talks about filling up your partner's "love tank" drip by drip through showing them love in their way. May your gas tanks and your love tanks be full as you learn to speak the language of your spouse.

---

http://www.5lovelanguages.com/profile/couples

Let's Re-Disc-over Our Love

Idea: Play Frisbee Golf.

Plan: Frisbee golf is taking the world by storm! Okay, okay, maybe not, but there are a few real Frisbee golf courses scattered around, and visiting one of those was the inspiration behind this date. Grab a Frisbee, or if you're a trained "frolfer," grab your bag of diversely-weighted discs, and head to the backyard.

If you don't have a backyard, you could do what we did and go to a park with a playground so our kids could play while we had our Frisbee golf date in a field right next to them. Decide together what your targets will be for each hole and get throwing! Keep score by counting every throw it takes to reach the target, and like golf, lowest score wins.

Production Help: If you're doing this in your backyard, utilize the space you have by adding challenges to each hole. You can do this by shooting the Frisbee between your deck's supporting beams, making the Frisbee land on top of a bush to win the hole, standing a hula hoop against a fence for a target, or by mixing up your stances with mandatory backward throws, or under-the-leg flings.

Throw caution (and your Frisbee) to the wind as you get adventurous with your homemade frolf course.

It's Time to Heat Things Up

Idea: Build a campfire.
Jeff's Fave Five

Burn the Evidence: Just like your 70-year-old neighbor, one of my guilty pleasures is the TV show *20/20*. You know, the one about murders gone terribly wrong (or right, depending on how you look at it). This date idea came when I was in the thick of a *20/20* marathon.

We had gone all around town trying to find a place to make a campfire with our son, Eli. Each fire-pitted park or national forest was annoyingly occupied. We searched for over an hour for a place to golden up a mallow. It wasn't happening.

Discouraged but determined, Jeff took all of our fire-starting supplies straight from the back of our car into our backyard. Jeff began clearing out the weeds from a dirted area and began teepeeing twigs. "Are we allowed to make a fire in our backyard?" I questioned, "And so close to the house?"

Jeff quietly replied, "I don't care what the fire codes are. I told Eli we're making a fire tonight, so we're going to make a fire." The perfect crime.

We had our fire. We put the fire out. The house didn't burn down. The cops weren't called. However, all the episodes of *20/20* whizzed through my mind as we finished the night by pulling shovels from the garage and scooping dirt onto the evidence of our evening while Jeff solemnly said, "There. Now nobody has to know what happened."

How many episodes of *20/20* had I seen where a neighbor saw the other one in the backyard with shovels and overheard them say, "Now nobody has to know what happened?"

I prayed for the next three months we wouldn't be wrongly accused of murder. I foresaw our mostly-innocent fire turning into heated TV appearances of us versus the neighbor who looked out their window at just the right (or wrong, depending on how you look at it) time.

Idea: A backyard (and a lenient city fire code) is all that's needed for this evening of at-home camping. Make yourselves a little backyard campfire to roast marshmallows, hot dogs, Starburst, or maybe even try out a s'mone (s'more cone–fill a waffle cone with chocolate chips, candy, and all sorts of yummy ice cream toppings; wrap it in tinfoil and throw it on the fire for a few minutes for a delicious ooey gooey campfire treat).

You camping diehards out there could throw a tent up in the backyard to double up on the convenient camping experience–but with the benefit of nearby flushing toilets–while the rest of us can instead choose to enjoy the thrill of a fire without the risk of the bears. (Hey, I don't know what roams my backyard at night.)

Alternate Idea: No backyard? No problem! Use the broiler in your oven to roast marshmallows for s'mores or s'mones. Enjoy them to the crackling of a YouTube fire displayed on your TV.

Huddle up in sleeping bags in front of your imitation fire for ghost stories and junk food. Reminisce about your favorite camp songs from when you were young. Bust out the boondoggle and friendship bracelets to fully simulate an evening in the mountains.

YouTube It: Check out these YouTube videos for a bracelet tutorial or a TV fire:

- **Virtual Campfire by Virtual Fireplace:** Virtual Campfire with Crackling Fire Sounds (HD), https://www.youtube.com/watch?v=iz7wtTO7roQ
- **Friendship Bracelets by Red Ted Art:** How to Make DIY Friendship Bracelets Beginners (Diagonal Pattern), https://www.youtube.com/watch?v=n2rq-btMNFI

Show Me The Money

Idea: Talk finances.

Buck Up: Listen. I don't like budgeting any more than you do. Which is why I don't budget. But I wish I did! And I know. Couples fight more about money than anything else, so me flaunting a night discussing money with your spouse as a great way to connect with each other is kind of like saying waving a red flag is a great way to connect with a bull. But, arguably, there will be a connection?

As often as I've heard money is the number one source of marital arguments, I've also heard marital couples enjoy making up after an argument. Let this be your opportunity to get all the feelings flying as you make a plan with your money. Because, let's face it, you will eventually need to graduate from these dates and actually leave the house every once in a while. What?!? Oh, now I'M THE BAD GUY?!? Somebody had to say it. Sheesh. Things are already getting heated.

Plan: It's time to talk about money. Open any and every account you have that shows your spending. I'm talking your bank account, your credit card account(s), PayPal, Venmo, the checkbook? (Hi, Grandma!) See where your money is going. Track where you spent the last month's worth of money to see your trends.

Decide what needs to stay and what can go. Assess. Remove. Clean it up! Make a plan! Get on the same page. Talk calmly and without judgment. View it as an open brainstorming session on how to make the most of what you've got.

Crash Cash Course: Take your date one step further by learning more about finances to be smarter with your money (and hopefully fight about it less, leading to unrestrained marital bliss). You could pick a podcast to begin listening to together. Here are a few to get you started:

- *Listen Money Matters*
- *The Dave Ramsey Show*
- *Afford Anything*
- *Radical Personal Finance*
- *The Side Hustle Show*
- *Stacking Benjamins*

Make a plan to abolish any debt. Find extra ways to save. Consider ways to make more money. Think about what talents or skills you have and how they could be monetized. We've made extra money by starting an Etsy shop, doing secret shopping, and driving for Amazon Flex. Get your creative juices and some extra cash flowing.

Relax, I've Got Your Back

Idea: Treat yourselves to a night at the spa.

Plan: Create an evening at the spa where bathtubs are hot tubs, dollar store face masks become luxurious skin treatments, and your spouse is suddenly a master masseuse. Light candles, pull out the sliced cucumbers, slather your faces in slime, care for each other's nails and cuticles, soak your feet in the tub, or spoil your spouse with a massage. (But maybe pass on the acupuncture treatments.)

Fatten Up the Plans: The danger of scrolling through Pinterest is that sometimes you come across a DIY skin treatment that encourages you to stick your feet in bags of lard. The Pinterest post flaunted impressive before and after pictures that were so convincing it caused me to plan a whole date night around it.

Be like us and skip the luxury (and price tag) of a professional spa. Instead, grab a Ziplock bag for each foot, a spoonful of Crisco for each bag, and giggle as much as we did as we slid our feet into goo. Secure each bag with a rubber band around the ankle, and then dip your feet in a piping hot bath to melt the Crisco and soak it into your overworked feet. After 15-20 minutes, unveil your silky smooth tootsies. The shocker of the night? This unconventional moisturizer actually worked!

I'm All On Board

Idea: Create vision boards.

A Vision is Born: Not listed in my recommended books for date night book group is *The Secret*. Not because I don't like it per se, but because I've never read it.

However, I have listened to a podcast called *By the Book* (one of my favorites by the way) where Jolenta Greenberg and Kristen Meinzer live by different self-help books for two weeks at a time. For one of their self-help experiments, they created vision boards while living by *The Secret*.

Before long, I had developed my own interpretation of the podcast's interpretation of a book I haven't even ever opened to create this mildly under-researched but undoubtedly entertaining date idea with all of you. Aren't we all here just for the entertainment anyway? Let's get vision boarding already!

Plan: Hunt down your old magazines, newspapers, weekly coupon mailers, old textbooks, or gather some writing utensils and a posterboard to create your life's vision. This could reflect goals, aspirations, desires, interests, dreams, anything positive you hope will come into your life. Find something that reflects your vision to add to the poster.

Do this as a couple or as individuals and spend time sharing your vision with your spouse. Hang up the poster for a motivational reminder of what you're working towards.

You're a Vision: Here's a clue to get you started—find a cute couple in the PennySaver to remind you of your admirable goal to save money while you save your relationship by dating each other at home! Man, you two are naturals.

Gimme A Pizza Your Heart

Idea: Make a pizza.

Plan: I know you love pizza because, who doesn't?!? What you might not know is you love to MAKE pizza! All the way down to the crust. Roll out a pizza, whip up some sauce, and have fun throwing on your own toppings. You could each make one and have a pizza-off, or combine your efforts into one magnificent pizza pie. This one makes a fun double date, or you can keep it as an always perfect one-on-one!

Bobby Flay's Pizza Dough

3 ½ - 4 cups bread flour (can substitute all purpose flour, bread flour makes crispier crust)
1 teaspoon sugar
1 envelope dry yeast
2 teaspoons salt
1 ½ cups warm water (around 110 degrees Fahrenheit)
2 tablespoons olive oil + 2 teaspoons

1. Combine flour, sugar, yeast and salt in the bowl of a stand mixer. While the mixer is running, add the water and 2 tablespoons of the oil and beat until the dough forms into a ball. If the dough is sticky, add additional flour, 1 tablespoon at a time, until the dough comes together in a solid ball. If the dough is too dry, add additional water, 1 tablespoon at a time. Scrape the dough onto a lightly floured surface and gently knead into a smooth, firm ball.

2. Grease a large bowl with the remaining 2 teaspoons olive oil, add the dough, cover the bowl with plastic wrap and put it in a warm area to let it double in size, about 1 hour. Turn the dough out onto a lightly floured surface and divide it into 2 equal pieces. Cover each with a clean kitchen towel or plastic wrap and let them rest for 10 minutes.

3. Bake in a 450-degree F oven for 8-10 minutes once sauce and toppings are in place.

PIZZA SAUCE

1 (14 1/2-ounce) can diced tomatoes, undrained
1 (6-ounce) can tomato paste
1 teaspoon sugar
1/2 teaspoon dried oregano
1/4 teaspoon garlic salt
1/2 teaspoon dried basil
Pinch of crushed red pepper

1. Combine all ingredients in food processor or blender and blend until desired consistency. I leave mine slightly chunky. You can adjust the seasonings to taste. This recipe is open to interpretation. Use what you like, taste it along the way and it is sure to be delicious!

---

https://www.melskitchencafe.com/homemade-pizza-sauce/
https://www.foodnetwork.com/recipes/bobby-flay/pizza-dough-recipe-1921714

Roses are Red, Violets are Blue, I'd Love to Go on a Date with You.

Idea: Write poetry.

One English assignment as a teen,
Left me staring at a blank computer screen.
Tasked to compile rhythmic phrases,
Into a book with many pages.
Completely unsure where I should start,
I became paralyzed, head to heart.
I silently stared at that stark screen,
Convinced I lacked a creative gene.
Class time ticked by with nothing to show.
The only thing in my head was "D'oh!"
I twitched, fidgeted, and perspired,
Felt everything except inspired.
Almost overcome by my agony,
'Til a poetic epiphany.
Think of what you care strongly about,
Arrange some words and then spit them out.
It can start sloppy, goofy or weird.
Just try them out, nothing to be feared.
I fumbled through things, mostly minute,
Until my writings were quite astute.
Soon rhymes were rolling off of my tongue;
A rag of words waiting to be wrung.
And so I say to you dear dater,
Do not be a poetry hater.
It might not be your cup of tea,
But remember, nor was it for me.

Which is why I left this here to see,
The realm of your possibility.

Plan: Had I known how influential my senior year Honors English class was going to be, I would have given my teacher a better parting gift than a "forget you!" as I walked out the doors of my high school on the last day of my senior year. Teenagers, amiright?

Along with forcing us to create a life list, we were also forced to release our inner poet–another challenge I'm going to extend to you! It may feel silly at first, but go with it. You could write one poem together or each write your own. I don't care how you do it; go ahead and get to it!

The Fantasy Suite?

Idea: Turn your house into a home-tel.

Plan: Consider me Chris Harrison, and consider this your long-awaited fantasy suite card. *Cue a magical transformation of you turning your house into a hotel!* Grab an air mattress (or a pile of blankets) and sleep in your living room or basement or somewhere other than your bedroom. With the right lighting (and a good attitude), you might feel as if you were staying overnight in a five star hotel.

Production Help: Try this date for an anniversary or special occasion. Order take-out to double as room service and live for a night like housekeeping will be knocking on your door in the morning to clean up after you. And then in the morning, knock on your own door to clean up after yourselves. Like the responsible adults that you are.

Pillow Talk: Since you'll be feeling like you're on your honeymoon as you're tucked away in a cozy hotel room, take the chance to play *The Newlywed Game*! Each of you takes a piece of paper and writes your name on one side with your spouse's name on the other. Flip your paper to whomever best fits the description using the questions below. When you get through these, come up with some of your own!

- Who is more likely to crack their phone screen?
- Who is a bigger diva?
- Who is a better cook?
- Who made the first move?
- Who is more accident prone?

- Who is a better dresser?
- Who takes out the trash more?
- Who is more likely to indulge in a pajama day?
- Who is more likely to run a marathon?
- Who has more street smarts?
- Who is more likely to get lost?
- Who said "I love you" first?
- Who is more likely to read a self-help book?
- Who has a better memory?
- Who is more likely to eat a whole pie in one sitting?
- Who is a bigger flirt?
- Who is a better dancer?
- Who is more likely to buy something from an infomercial?
- Who was a better student in high school?
- Who is more stubborn?
- Who is more likely to change a light bulb?
- Who is more likely to max out the credit card?
- Who is on their phone more?
- Who is a better driver?
- Who watches more TV?
- Who loves this book the most?
  Trick question. It's a tie!

Everything is Going to Be Croquet

Idea: Play croquet (or any lawn game).

Stake in the Game: The idol of my childhood was my 5-years-older-than-me brother, Abe. The only trouble was, these feelings were not at all reciprocated.

When Abe wasn't stealthily shaking salt into my hair, frantically finding firecrackers to attach to my bedroom door, or brazenly beheading my Barbies, he was shooing me off the front lawn while he and his friends played croquet.

Every summer, Abe and his friends religiously paced the lawn with mallets, balls, and what looked to me like a pile of broken wire hangers. With Abe being my sole source of determining what was cool, it became abundantly clear that croquet was at the top of the list. Followed closely by Weezer and the Ninja Turtles.

My dreams of one day playing croquet finally seemed possible when Abe left for college, suddenly making the croquet set cast aside in my parents' garage fair game. By then, none of my friends understood my urgency to master the mallet swing, so I was left with the game but no one to play it with.

I spent years hopelessly waiting for the opportune moment when both a croquet set and someone to play the sport with would become available to me at the same time.

So, to answer your original question, I guess you could say the reason I got married was so I would have a lifetime croquet partner who wouldn't run away from me or put salt in my hair. So far so good!

Plan: Unlike my older brother, I'm extending an invitation for you to play a game of croquet. If you don't have a croquet set, any lawn game will do. Round up horseshoes, volleyball, soccer, cornhole, ladder toss, bocce ball, Spikeball (double date!), or darts and enjoy a lively evening in the grass.

Production Help: Ask friends, family, neighbors, or your cool older brother if they have lawn games you could borrow. Plan ahead so you have time to check thrift stores, yard sales, or Amazon if you're willing to make a little investment in your dating life. (Weezer playlist optional.)

Just Give Me a Minute of Your Time

Idea: Have a face-off with *Minute-to-Win-It* challenges.
Sarah's Fave Five

Plan: Assemble a few *Minute-to-Win-It* games using things you already have around the house. We had seven games ready to go, providing just the right amount of variety while still allowing us enough time to go back and do the more challenging ones over again until we could complete them.

Production Help: Google is your best friend on this date. Also check out YouTube videos for visual instructions on nearly every challenge. Here are ten easy-to-assemble options:

(If you aren't familiar with Minute-to-Win-It, and if the title doesn't quite speak for itself, all of these challenges are to be completed in...one minute.)

Stack it Up: Stack 25 pennies using only one hand.

Defy Gravity: Using only one hand, keep two balloons in the air for the whole minute.

Speed Eraser: Place five mugs on a table. Bounce a pencil, eraser side down, on the table so that it flips into the mug. Get all five pencils in all five mugs to win this challenge.

This Blows: Place 15 paper/plastic disposable cups on the edge of a table. When the timer starts, blow up a balloon and use the escaping air to knock down the cups. Balloon can be blown up as many times as the clock allows.

Rapid Fire: Stack six plastic cups in a pyramid. By shooting a rubber band, knock down all the cups.

Johnny Apple Stack: Stack five apples on top of each other.

Card Ninja: Cut a watermelon in half and prop it up with the cut side facing the player. Using a deck of cards, throw them one by one at the watermelon until one sticks.

Stick the Landing: Flip a filled water bottle to get it to land right side up on a chair or table.

Breakfast Scramble: Cut the front of a cereal box into 20 squares ahead of time. Solve the puzzle before time runs out.

Shoe Fly Shoe: Line up a bunch of shoes. Using only one foot, flip one of the shoes onto a table.

DREAM WITH ME

Idea: Make a few goals.
Try this one for New Year's

Plan: This is a great date for resolutions in January, but if you're like me, I think any time is a great time to assess your life and set some goals! They can be personal, couple goals, or a little bit of both!

Discover each other's hidden dreams and aspirations and find a way to help each other achieve those dreams! Reflect on the past year and recognize the feats you've accomplished. Share with each other the things you aspire to work on, and write down the goals you come up with.

Get SMART About It: At the start of every year my dad obsessively encouraged my siblings and me to set 4-7 goals. There was no getting around it. The first Sunday of January was always goal-setting day. We were pestered by our dad until we came up with an approved list of things to work on.

After we had our list, my dad would grade each goal to assess if it was a "SMART" goal. This got a lot of eye rolls out of us as we tried to quickly work through the assignment by writing down things like "Don't smoke," (a favorite made by my brother at the age of 8) or "Make my bed every day," (an idea eagerly whispered to us by our mother). My dad would exasperatingly (because we reviewed this all the time) ask, "Is this a SMART goal?" "...Yes?" We would all sheepishly answer as we anticipated the inevitable lecture.

The lecture consisted of an idea from an Organizational Behavior class my dad took in college that he quickly became 100% converted to. In fact, he's here to give you the lecture himself right now!

"Dad! Hi! Welcome to my book. Be kind to my readers and tell them how SMART they are!"

"Hi all, Glen here. You can check the quality of your goals by running them through these guidelines:"

- **Specific** (simple, sensible, significant)
○ Be a better spouse. –> Do one intentionally kind thing for my spouse each week.
- **Measurable** (meaningful, motivating)
○ Date my spouse. –> Date my spouse once a week.
- **Aggressive** (agreed, attainable)
○ Be a perfect husband. –> Set aside 10 minutes each day to connect with my wife.
- **Realistic** (reasonable, realistic, and results-based)
○ Make my husband happy. –> Do one thoughtful thing for my husband every day.
- **Timed** (time-based, time limited, timely, time-sensitive)
○ Date my spouse from my house. –> Try 30 of the date ideas from this book.

"Thanks, Dad. Oh, and sorry for all those times I rolled my eyes at you."

---

https://courses.lumenlearning.com/suny-hccc-orgbehavior/chapter/6-3-motivating-employees-through-goal-setting/

HUMOR ME

Idea: Create your own comedy club.

A man's main job is to protect his woman from her desire to "get bangs" every other month.
-Dax Shepard

Before you marry a person, you should first make them use a computer with slow internet to see who they really are.
-Will Ferrell

My wife's gotten really lazy, or as she calls it, "pregnant."
-Jim Gaffigan

Laughin' with Gaffigan: If I had to pinpoint the moment I fell in love with Jim Gaffigan, it would probably be when I was listening to his book *Dad is Fat*. I downloaded it without knowing anything about my guy Gaff.

The relatable humor caught me completely off guard in all the most hilarious ways. I grew to love Jim so much that when he came to Salt Lake City, I did the unthinkable; I hired a babysitter and demanded we actually leave the house for date night.

By the end of the night, Jeff and I had sore cheeks, a borderline ab workout, and an overall sense of lightness about life. I became even more obsessed with Jim. I sought out his comedy routines on Netflix and YouTube as my favorite way to unwind for the next few weeks after seeing his show.

I was thrilled one evening to find a new release from Jim appear in my queue. As I began watching, it was immediately apparent that it was basically the exact same show we had just gone to see, released mere weeks after we had shelled out the big bucks to get a babysitter and see him in person.

Watching Jim's show at home, in my pajamas, in my bed, for free, was definitely more satisfying than getting all dressed up to watch him tell some jokes while sitting on a hard seat in a cramped auditorium where I could barely see him.

That was the moment I decided even though Jim is kind of my favorite famous person, I think I'll sit the rest of them out. From my bed. Two weeks later on Netflix. And Jim, if there's anyone who can understand this opinion, I know it's you.

Plan: Your house is now a cozy comedy club. Grab some popcorn. Pour yourselves a fun drink with a napkin as a coaster. Dim the lights, and shine a spotlight on your TV to set the stage for your favorite comedian. Netflix has a whole slew to choose from. Many of them can get quite explicit, so I'm going to stick with my recommendation of Jim.

You could also create your own line-up through YouTube by trying out different comedians, giving the hook to the ones you don't like while discovering new people you enjoy.

***Bachelor* Style:** You know how at least once a season *The Bachelor* likes to fill an auditorium up with people and then breaks the news to the inexperienced contestants that they have to perform stand-up in front of an impatient audience waiting to laugh?

You could play this date that way as well. If you're feeling confident and a bit adventurous, challenge each other to a round of stand-up to see how well you...stand up against each other. Here's to hoping your jokes are better than mine!

Is Our Love Authentic?

Idea: Make a meal from the country of your choice.

Passport to Paris: (<– A quiet nod to my favorite Mary-Kate and Ashley Olsen movie.)

It was after my brother (the croquet one) had just returned from an extravagant Icelandic adventure when I first decided I needed to get out more. I needed to get out of my house, and I needed to get out of the country.

Unsatisfied with my lack of culture, yet undeterred by my lack of money, I made plans–plans for Paris. Judging by my newest Pinterest board filled with stunning shots of the Eiffel Tower, beginners' lists of frequently-used French phrases, and every must-try French dish that didn't involve a fry, you could be certain I was Paris bound.

I stared longingly at my computer screen filled with images of quaint red-and-white striped cafe awnings, fancy French natives flaunting effortless style and class, and cozy shops offering gourmet carbs at every corner.

Without a second thought about our finances, Jeff and I went to Paris. Dressed in our finest clothes, we sat cozily beneath an awning at a little cafe called Mi Amor. We ate a mouth-watering roast chicken with a had-to-have-it baguette, complete with a side of green beans that only the French could make taste that good.

Our meal was complete when our waitress brought out a slice of cheesecake to savor as we looked out the window of the cafe in awe at the Eiffel Tower. It was magical.

Then my mom...er...the waitress took our plates away. Eli woke up, so I abruptly stood up to reinsert his binky, spilling a greasy green bean on my high school prom dress. Jeff was left to stare at the picture of the Eiffel Tower I had printed off the computer and stuck to the window as he waited underneath the red-and-white awning I had crafted from a cardboard box and taped to the wall.

As I ran back downstairs to return to Jeff after taking care of our son, I saw the Julia Child recipes strewn about the kitchen. That was the moment I gave myself a pat on the back because for a small moment we had escaped it all. We had weaseled our way into France without the passport or the price tag.

Plan: Is it inauthentic to pretend you're in another country making their traditional meals using substitute items from your local Walmart and having Google translate your dinner conversation into the native tongue of your evening imitations? Yes? I beg to differ! It's called learning about another culture in an affordable way, by golly!

Imaginatively travel to another country with your spouse. Learn about the country. Speak a little of the language. Virtually visit the tourist hot spots, and indulge in many authentic laughs along the way.

This idea is one you can have a lot of fun with. You can execute this as intricately or as simply as you want. You could go the Sarah way and create cardboard awnings for your living room, print pictures of your would-be destination, and recreate from scratch authentic dishes. Alternatively, you could also order Chinese take-out and eat it with a fork like a rebel.

You're the (Pac)Man

Idea: Create a night at the arcade.

Plan: If you have access to a Nintendo, XBox, Playstation, or any old computer will do, have an "Arcade Night" by playing video games together. I prefer the old school video games for date night to keep things light and fun.

Find your childhood Nintendo 64 and race through a few rounds of Mario Kart, battle it out on Super Smash Brothers, or see who can snatch the most stars in Mario Party.

Production Help: If you don't have a gaming console, check out these websites that offer free games: friv.com, playretrogames.com, or free80sarcade.com.

I Can Trump That: Now I'm not talking about the president. I'm talking about the card game, Rook. My husband and I went through a few months of being obsessed with this card game. The trouble is, it takes four players to play, and as newlyweds, we were rarely in the company of fellow "Rookies."

In desperation, we discovered there was an online community of Rook enthusiasts like us who had developed a (very low budget) website to play with like-minded folks who were all chasing after the same bird.

We were in school at the time and were often found in the campus computer lab caught up in the cyber shuffle of Rook cards. It was a thrill to lose ourselves in the shared passion of a   newly-learned   card   game.   Those later-than-was-responsible game nights are now some of our fondest memories of our first year of marriage.

You might not find yourselves spending all hours of this date night locked up in a college computer lab, forgetting to eat meals and go to the bathroom, but I am willing to bet on the kitty you can find at least one game that draws you in. So get playing!

(Are you a Rookie, too? Maybe I'll find you online at www.duelboard.com!)

I'm Do-nuts for You

Idea: Make donuts.

The Way to My Heart: I knew Jeff was the one for me one Valentine's Day when he thoughtfully came home from work with a dozen beautiful, perfectly arranged, fragrant-filled...donuts.

It's reassuring I had feelings of him being the right one for me because we were two years into our marriage, but still, it's nice to get those little confirmations. Yes, some girls melt at the sight of a man with a handful of flowers, but I'll take my romantic gestures in the form of glazed carbs, please. They last longer that way.

Plan: Have you made donuts before?! I didn't think so. Like me, you probably didn't even realize you COULD make donuts. But you CAN! And they're FUN! We actually did this date two times because we loved it so much.

Search for recipes online or use the baked variety we used below. One night we made baked; the next night we tried fried. All variations were DELICIOUS! Don't forget to cook the donut holes for bite-sized yummy-ness!

Production Help: For the baked version, I made the dough ahead of time so we didn't have to wait for it to rise the first hour. This allowed us to spend the date doing more of the interactive parts of the process: rolling, cutting, and icing our delicious date night delicacy.

Baked Donuts

1 1/3 cups warm milk, 95 to 105 degrees
2 teaspoons instant yeast
2 tablespoons butter
2/3 cup granulated sugar
2 large eggs
5 cups all-purpose flour
A pinch or two of nutmeg, freshly grated
1 teaspoon salt

Icing Ingredients

1/4 cup milk
1 teaspoon vanilla extract
2 cups powdered sugar

Directions

1. Place the warm milk in the bowl of an electric mixer. Stir in the yeast and sugar. Add the butter. Mix the eggs, flour, nutmeg, and salt. Beat the dough with the dough hook attachment (or with a wooden spoon and eventually your hands) for 2-3 minutes at medium speed.

2. Adjust the dough texture by adding flour a few tablespoons at a time or more milk. The dough should pull away from the sides of the bowl and be very soft and smooth but still slightly sticky – don't over-flour!

3. Knead the dough for a few minutes (again, by mixer or by hand) and then transfer the dough to a lightly greased bowl. Cover the bowl and let the dough rise for about an hour or until it has doubled in size (the exact time will depend on the temperature of your kitchen).

4. Punch down the dough and roll it out to about 1/2-inch thickness on a lightly floured counter. Using a donut cutter or a 2-3 inch circle cookie cutter, cut out circles in the dough.
5. Carefully transfer the circles to a parchment- or silpat-lined baking sheet and stamp out the smaller inner circles using a smaller cutter. Be sure to make the holes large enough that as the donuts rise again and bake, they don't fill in the donut hole with the puffiness of the dough.
6. Cover the tray with lightly greased plastic wrap. Let the donuts rise for about another 45 minutes, until they are puffed and nearly doubled.
7. Bake in 375 degree F oven until the bottoms are just golden, 8 to 10 minutes. Start checking the donuts around minute 8. They should be pale on top, not golden and browned, and barely baked through.
8. Remove the donuts from the oven and let cool for 1-2 minutes. Combine icing ingredients. Dip each donut in the icing one at a time. Enjoy!

---

https://www.melskitchencafe.com/baked-doughnuts/

Are We in Tune with Each Other?

Idea: Play *Name That Tune.*
Jeff's Fave Five

YouTune: What started out as me trying to remember the theme song to one of my favorite childhood shows, *Clarissa Explains It All*, quickly turned into a YouTube search war of Jeff and me playing clips from various TV musical intros to see if the other person could guess which show it belonged to.

Plan: Pull up a method of playing music (think YouTube) and test your tune-naming skills. Search for old TV sitcom theme songs, one-hit wonders, or maybe even video game music. Then slowly reveal them to each other second by second until the other person can shout out the show/song/game the music belongs to.

Don't underestimate the amount of time this simple game can occupy. This date will send you singing down memory lane as you reminisce about your various modes of entertainment from years past.

Let's Be Lab Rats

Idea: Complete an activity from John Gottman's book *The Seven Principles of Making Marriage Work.*

Plan: If you're at all interested in love and marriage, which judging by how far you've made it into this book, I can tell you definitely ARE, you'll love the book *The Seven Principles of Making Marriage Work* by John Gottman.

Gottman spent thirty years observing married couples for one week at a time in a "Love Lab" and has reported his findings in his book. As you read, you'll find questions and activities to complete with your spouse. Spend an evening creating your own "Love Lab" through activities in the book and learn what's making your marriage work!

Production Help: Our favorite activity from Gottman's book is the Love Map 20 Questions Game.

Instructions: Play this game together in the spirit of laughter and gentle fun. Each of you should take a piece of paper and pen. Together, randomly decide on 20 numbers between 1 and 60. Write the numbers down in a column on the left-hand side of your paper.

Below is a list of numbered questions. Beginning with the top of your column, match the numbers you chose with the corresponding questions. Each of you should ask your partner this question.

If your partner answers correctly, he or she receives the number of points indicated for that question, and you receive one point. If your spouse answers incorrectly, neither of you receive any points. The winner is the person with the higher score after you've both answered all twenty questions.

1. Name my two closest friends. (2)
2. Who is my favorite band/musician? (2)
3. What was I wearing when we first met? (2)
4. Name one of my hobbies. (3)
5. Where was I born? (1)
6. What stresses am I facing right now? (4)
7. Describe in detail what I did today, or yesterday. (4)
8. When is my birthday? (1)
9. What is the date of our anniversary (or engagement)? (1)
10. Who is my favorite relative? (2)
11. What is my fondest unrealized dream? (5)
12. What is my favorite flower? (2)
13. What is one of my greatest fears or disaster scenario? (3)
14. What is my favorite time of day? (3)
15. What makes me feel most complete? (4)
16. What turns me on? (3)
17. What is my favorite meal? (2)
18. What is my favorite way to spend the evening? (2)
19. What is my favorite color? (1)
20. What personal improvements do I want to make in my life? (4)
21. What kind of present would I like best? (2)
22. What was one of my best childhood experiences? (2)
23. What was my favorite vacation? (2)
24. What is one of my favorite ways to be soothed? (4)

25. Who is my greatest source of support (besides you)? (3)

26. What is my favorite sport? (2)

27. What do I most like to do with time off? (2)

28. What is one of my favorite weekend activities? (2)

29. What is my favorite getaway place? (3)

30. What is my favorite movie? (2)

31. What are some of the important events coming up in my life? How do I feel about them? (4)

32. What are some of my favorite ways to work out? (2)

33. Who was my best friend in childhood? (3)

34. What is one of my favorite magazines? (2)

35. Name one of my major rivals or enemies. (3)

36. What would I consider my dream job? (4)

37. What do I fear the most? (4)

38. Who is my least favorite relative? (3)

39. What is my favorite holiday? (2)

40. What kinds of books do I most like to read? (3)

41. What is my favorite TV show? (2)

42. Am I right-handed or left-handed? (2)

43. What am I most sad about? (4)

44. Name one of my concerns or worries. (4)

45. What medical problems do I worry about? (2)

46. What was my most embarrassing moment? (3)

47. What was my worst childhood experience? (3)

48. Name two of the people I admire most (4)

49. What was my high school's mascot. (3)

50. Of all the people we both know, who do I like least? (3)

51. What is one of my favorite desserts? (2)

52. What is my social security number? (2)

53. Name one of my favorite novels. (2)

54. What is my favorite restaurant? (2)

55. What are two of my aspirations, hopes, wishes? (4)

56. Do I have a secret ambition? What is it? (4)
57. What foods do I hate? (2)
58. What is my favorite animal? (2)
59. What is my favorite song? (2)
60. Which sports team is my favorite? (2)

Gottman, John and Nan Silver: *The Seven Principles For Making Marriage Work: A Practical Guide From the Country's Foremost Relationship Expert* (New York: Three Rivers Press, 1999).

It's Time To Get in the Swing of Things

Idea: Learn how to swing dance!
Sarah's Fave Five

The Warm Up: If I were to pick one date plan I was most nervous to reveal to Jeff, it would easily be this one. We're the kind of people who can be found hugging the wall at any social gathering where dancing is involved.

My husband and I are well aware of our awkward musical body movements and general lack of rhythm. Any kind of dancing leaves me looking as awkward as a giraffe on stilts. I have no coordination, little sense of rhythm, and my ability to remember a repetitive set of steps is nonexistent, yet the desire to learn some moves lies deep within me and is trying its hardest to dance itself out.

How could I get a personal dance instructor to give me a lesson without the embarrassment of them seeing my unskilled-ness? Hello, YouTube. I had the great idea to do a quick YouTube search to see if there were any beginner dance classes Jeff and I could tap along to. Sure enough, there were plenty! We picked a beginner swing dancing class and got stepping.

What ended up being one of our favorite dates of the year continued through the week as our after-work hellos became enhanced with spontaneous bursts of choreographed dance steps. Our table clearing after dinner suddenly included advanced, spin-infused side-stepping. Our paths could no longer cross without jazz hands somehow involved. Seriously. Give this one a try. You might be surprised at how well the stilted giraffe within you can bust a move.

Plan: What are you waiting for? Grab your partner, clear the living room, find a televised instructor, and get swingin'! With your newly-acquired respect for people who can skillfully wiggle their bodies, cool down by watching *Footloose*, *Dirty Dancing*, or an episode of *Dancing with the Stars*.

Production Help: We used this video to get our dancing career started:

The Swing Dancer: "The Swing Dancer Series" Learning how to swing dance in less than 30 minutes.

---

https://www.youtube.com/watch?v=drLc7eYNw-E

Show Me Some 'Tude

Idea: Make gratitude lists.
Try this around Thanksgiving!

From Attitude to Gratitude: Soon after we had our third baby, Jeff and I began to notice we were bickering with each other quite a bit more than usual. Our tones had turned sassy, our interactions short, and our annoyances high.

We sat down one night to hash out our differences and to see if we could get on the same page. As we started talking, it became clear that with the added responsibilities, we were both doing more than we were used to, feeling overworked, but also feeling underappreciated by each other.

Basically what it boiled down to was gratitude. We weren't taking the time to notice efforts made by the other person, we weren't feeling grateful for each other, and we definitely weren't expressing appreciation to each other.

We decided to focus on A) all hands on deck; everyone pitch in as much as possible, and then B) express gratitude to each other whenever we saw our spouse do absolutely anything for the greater good of our family.

That was all it took! What felt like a big wedge between Jeff and me was resolved simply by taking time to think positively about each other and by verbalizing our moments of gratitude.

Plan: Spend the night appreciating each other. This could be done by filling up a thank you note with spousal gratefulness. You could each make a list of 10 things the other person did in the last week that you appreciated but never got around to acknowledging. You could talk about attributes, skills, and qualities you're grateful your spouse has.

Production Help: If you plan this date in November, you could also grab a pumpkin and a Sharpie and scribble your appreciation for each other all over the pumpkin to serve as a reminder of your gratitude for your spouse through the whole month.

Thanks, Researchers: Still skeptical a little "thank you" can make a big difference? Ted Futris, an associate professor at the College of Family and Consumer Sciences at the University of Georgia conducted a study which found:

"When couples are stressed about making ends meet, they are more likely to engage in negative ways–they are more critical of each other and defensive, and they can even stop engaging or withdraw from each other, which can then lead to lower marital quality. Gratitude, however, can interrupt this cycle and help couples overcome negative communication patterns in their relationship."

I guess the only thing left to do is to conduct your own experiment and see if you have the same results!

---

https://news.uga.edu/research-links-gratitude-positive-marital-outcomes-1015/

Don't Brush Me Off Tonight

Idea: Try watercoloring.

Make a Splash: I warmed you up with a straightforward paint-by-numbers, we explored color combos and shading with coloring books, and now it's time to make a splash as we dive into water...coloring.

Plan: The one thing that always makes it onto the back-to-school supplies list, yet the one thing that longingly stares at elementary-aged kids all year, is the overachieving and tragically underused watercolor set. Well watercolors, you're finally getting your chance!

Dig through your child's art supplies for the probably unopened paint pallet. You can also buy more mature (and expensive) versions if you have an interest in pursuing painting (or if you feel uneasy about breaking into your child's belongings). After that, all you need is a sheet of paper, and you're ready to take a dip in the water—without the hassle of a swimsuit.

Butterfly Stroke: Here are some quick ideas of things to paint to get you started:

Your house	Landscape
Your family	Portrait of your spouse
Fruit/Food	A favorite quote

Do We Fit Together?

Idea: Have a puzzle race.

Sibling Puzzlery: When you're eight years old and your sister is fifteen, trust me when I say you DO NOT want to engage in a puzzle race with her. The stakes are high (bragging rights), her fingers are nimble, and that age gap is just the disadvantage you can never overcome.

Lucky for you, you didn't marry your older sister (...making some bold assumptions here). You married your spouse–who may have nimble fingers and an age advantage, but my guess is this could still be a fair game.

Plan: Hunt down two puzzles of equal pieces and difficulty level. If you aren't the proud owner of a pair of puzzles, check the dollar store, a second-hand store, or Walmart.

Regular puzzle rules apply (...are there puzzle rules?) with the added thrill of going head to head against your spouse for an amped-up, high-intensity, speed-infused puzzle race. Shake the boxes, dump the pieces, and the race is on!

It Feels Muggy in Here

Idea: Design your own mugs.

Plan: For this date you will need a permanent marker and a dollar store mug. Decorate the mug! You could make the mugs for each other or each make your own. Scribble all over that ceramic until your design is complete. Allow designs to dry overnight and then a 30-minute bask in a 350-degree oven will lock the ink in place for years' worth of mug-sipping memories.

It's Getting Hot in Here: Your mugs don't have to be the only ones heating things up in the kitchen. By that I mean whip up some hot chocolate while you wait for your ink to set. Here's a simple one-mug recipe for hot chocolate:

Hot Choco-Date

2 tablespoons unsweetened cocoa powder
1-2 tablespoons sugar (depending on how sweet you like it)
1 cup milk or any combination of milk, half-and-half, or cream
1/4 teaspoon vanilla extract

Directions: Whisk together the cocoa, sugar, and 2 tablespoons of milk in a saucepan over medium-low heat until cocoa and sugar are dissolved. Whisk in the rest of the milk and heat it over medium heat until hot then add vanilla.

---

https://www.epicurious.com/recipes/food/views/simple-hot
-cocoa-for-one-369469

At Your Service

Idea: Serve someone.
Great for the Christmas season!

Wrapped Up in Service: You'll usually find me urging you to get wrapped up in your spouse and to focus all of your love and attention on him/her. This week we're changing it up. I want you to forget your spouse. And forget yourself. Instead, get wrapped up in a good cause.

Jeff and I got wrapped up in The Burrito Project, a group that donates burritos every weekday evening to the homeless. We were able to help wrap hundreds of burritos, and then we hand-delivered the burritos to those in need. It's true, a portion of our date was not done at home, but there are plenty of ways to serve within the walls of your own home.

Plan: Use your date night as a chance to look outside yourself and find something you can do to help someone else. You could assemble 12 Days of Christmas gifts for a neighbor, make treats for a friend, or tie fleece blankets for a local hospital.

Look online to find ideas of things you can do in your area to help those around you. Spend the evening growing more in love with your spouse as together you share your love with someone in need.

Just Serve: When we did this date, we found an idea by using the JustServe app. You can also find ideas on the website: www.JustServe.org. To give you an idea of what you might find, here's a list of a variety of at-home service options in my area:

- Making bedazzled flowers for wigs to donate to The Magic Yarn Project
- Assembling hygiene/food kits for refugees
- Cleaning your pantry of unused food to donate to a local food pantry
- Making beanies for boys battling cancer
- Tying fleece blankets for local hospital
- Making finger puppets for children at a local women's shelter

Will You Hang with Me?

Idea: Make Christmas ornaments.

Putting "The Bomb" in Tannenbaum: Some families use the Christmas season to showcase their decorating abilities by turning their house into an aesthetically-pleasing tinsel bomb of color-coordinated ribbons and thoughtfully-themed knick knacks.

The family I grew up in donned our tree exclusively with whatever glue-smeared creations my siblings and I brought home from elementary school. But you wanna know what's kind of crazy? I think I prefer my tree to yours, Mrs. Jones.

Every year as we pulled all the handmade ornaments of Christmases past out of the storage box, we would giggle, awww, and nostalgiate (not a real word, but it should be). Then we would continue on with all of our sentimental feelings each time we would sit by the tree to watch it spin through the memories of our childhood one tacky ornament at a time. (Yes, my parents' Christmas tree spins, further solidifying my point that they're obviously doing everything right in the Christmas tree department.)

Plan: Make your own Christmas ornaments! We have made this a yearly tradition in our home to give us a tree full of fun memories to look back on with a smile each December.

You could use salt dough and cookie cutters, a popsicle stick and a marker, a glob of glue with eyes and call him a melted snowman once dried, a small picture frame with your family's silhouettes inside, a bead and pipe cleaner candy cane, an unmelted snowman made from a light bulb, or take your pick from any Pinterest board across America.

Nostalgiate Dough

2 cups flour
1 cup salt
1 cup water

Directions: Mix salt and flour. Add water. Knead 5-7 minutes. Allow to air dry or put in oven at 325 degrees for 30 minutes.

---

http://www.geniuskitchen.com/recipe/salt-dough-113757

How Well Do You Know Me?

Idea: Buy each other themed gifts.

Try this one out for an anniversary, holiday, or special occasion!

Plan: Show how much you care by getting your spouse little gifts that represent him/her. This one takes a little preparation, so plan in advance. Sit down with your spouse a week before your date to pick three gift categories. For example, you might pick books, a fragrance, and something free.

Spend the week on the lookout for a gift to fill each category for your spouse. When you meet for your date, you will each give one thing from each category. In our example, I might get a cookbook I've had my eye on, my favorite lotion, and an end table my husband's parents were getting rid of. Take time to talk about why you picked the things you did and the stories behind what it took to track them down.

Production Help: Look over these category suggestions to get your gift juices flowing:

T-shirt	Second-hand/Free	Home Decor
Book	Candy	Accessory
Fragrance	Picture	Poem/Writing
Music	Movie Rental	Homemade
Toiletry	Snack	Meme/GIF

Get Wrapped Up in Each Other: You may want to consider doing this idea for Christmas. I have a friend who exchanges gifts with her husband on Christmas Eve after the kids go to bed. This way she and her husband can have a quiet moment to focus on each other before the toy assembling, breakfast making, and wrapping paper vacuuming of Christmas consumes their morning.

Take the chance to celebrate with your spouse so you can relish in the thought and effort you each put into your gift preparations.

Let's Make a Heart Beat

Idea: Make a music video.

Beating Around the Bush: I made it this far into a book about marriage without even remotely beginning to meddle in your sex life. You're welcome. I cherish the trust you've given me as your source of wholesome, realistic, and instagrammable (heeeey #housedates) moments.

I didn't drag you along this far to turn on you now. This date idea in no way involves making a baby. Unless you grow to love the music video you're about to create so much that you forever refer to it as your "baby," which I can't promise won't happen. Everybody exhale. There you go. Onto the baby-making-less date.

Plan: If Rebecca Black did nothing more than prove to the world that absolutely anyone is capable of making a music video, we need to thank her for that. Without her, we might not have a date tonight. And after all...date night does usually land on a Friday, so...

To make this music video, you could come up with your own song (Rebecca Black style), you could make a parody of an existing song (The Holderness Family style), or you could insert your own dance moves/videography into an existing song (Jeff and Sarah style). You could even use some of your favorite pictures to make a slideshow set to music.

Dress up, change wardrobes, mix up the scenery, pull in the neighbors as back-up dancers? Once you have taken all the video clips, you can easily string them together with the free app FilmoraGo. You can also use more complex video editing software on a computer. (I like to use iMovie on my Mac. Try Windows Movie Maker for PCs.)

Video Scrapbook: We have a tradition of making a music video every time we go on vacation. We take little video clips throughout our trip and then string them together to create a memory-filled music video, forever capturing all the little moments of our adventures together.

You could try this option for a less-showy version of this date. Spend the days/weeks leading up to this date intentionally capturing little moments you spend together.

Hey, you could even take videos of yourselves every date night! As the crowning moment of your house dating, you can seal all your dates together for a year's worth of memories in a video scrapbook. That might be the best idea in this whole book. Am I the only one tearing up?!?

After The Final Rose

Chris Harrison: "Hello. Welcome to tonight's episode of 'After the Final Rose.' If you'll remember, this season had endless dramatic highs and lows. Let's bring out our couple to see if they've managed the nearly impossible feat of staying together once the helicopters fly away, the cameras turn off, and the dinners have a price tag. Come on out, you two!"

Bachelor Couple: "Hi. Hello. Oh wow, so many people. Hi! How are you? I love you, too! Oh. This is so overwhelming. Thank you. Thanks."

Chris Harrison: "Welcome back! It's so fun to see you again. Now, when we last left you, you were happy, in love, and recently engaged. I know it can be hard when the cameras turn off to keep the love alive, especially because you were stuck at home, ensuring no one saw you together before the show aired. Historically, this takes a toll on couples."

Bachelor Couple: "Yeah. It got really difficult as soon as the cameras turned off. We were on the brink of a breakup before our friend gave us this book, *Date Your Spouse From Your House.* It totally turned our world upside down! We saw that even though we had to spend a few months locked away from the public eye, we could make our own fun as we intentionally spent time together."

Chris Harrison: "Wow. What a great idea! So wait," *looks dramatically at the audience,* "does this mean you're still together?"

Bachelor Couple: "And stronger than ever! We may have met on *The Bachelor*, but we fell in love as we chose to make time for each other week after week."

Chris Harrison: "I think I'm going to start recommending that book to all the contestants!"

"Sarah, wake up." Jeff nudged me after I fell asleep watching *The Bachelor*, "Let's go to bed."

"Okay," I mumbled as I rolled off the couch and walked up to our room with a sense of enlightenment. "You know how I used to think it would be awesome to have a love life like those people on *The Bachelor*?"

"Yeah," he catered to my groggy questioning.

"Now I think they could take a page out of our book."

About the Author

Sarah Excell hasn't always written love notes. Her career started at age 8 when her mother tragically refused to let her play outside in the sprinkler. As a passive-aggressive way to deal with her disappointment, Sarah used her budding interest in writing to furiously scribble the first of what her family would lovingly refer to as "hate notes."

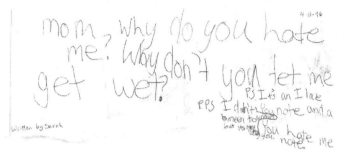

(Mom why do you hate me? Why don't you let me get wet?
P.S. It's an I love you note and a you hate me note.
P.P.S. I didn't meant to scream but it's hard living with you.)

While her passion for writing never died, the hate notes eventually did. Sarah's family knew she was in love when her writing became nonthreatening after meeting Jeff in college. Shortly after getting married, Sarah continued writing by starting a blog to capture the stories of her growing family.

After ten years of marriage and blog posts, Sarah now lives in Salt Lake City with Jeff and their four boys. Together they love to hike, play with Legos, bake cookies, visit parks, and (when Sarah's mom lets them) run through the sprinklers.